Thames & Hudson

Tank
Tel +44 (0)20 7434 0110
Fax +44 (0)20 7434 9232
mail@tankmagazine.com

Edited by Masoud Golsorkhi and Andreas Laeufer

First published in the United Kingdom in 2002 by Thames & Hudson Ltd,
181A High Holborn, London WC1V 7QX

www.thamesandhudson.com

British Library Cataloguing-in-Publication Data
A catalogue record for this book is available from the British Library

ISBN 0-500-28366-4

Printed and bound in Thailand

In 1998, a group of friends started having secret meetings at which they exchanged little-known facts about the publications for which they designed, photographed and wrote. On the whole, magazine publishing was consumer led, and the same ideas and stories were shamelessly reproduced over and over. During these late-night gatherings, the names of classic titles were invoked like talismans. Inspiration, once a byword in magazine publishing was all but forgotten by the 1990s. Paradoxically, as the technological revolution made the world smaller and enabled greater access for all, the scope of magazine publishing narrowed drastically.

tank was born out of a deeply held belief that ideas – in pictures, words and signs – should have dominion over commercial and PR concerns. A visually led publication that eschews easily consumed formulae, **tank** is one of the first magazines to avoid fashion's self-justifying 'clubbiness' and instead prioritize concept originality. The juxtaposition of fashion that resembles art and art that resembles fashion reinvigorates and electrifies both media. For the first time since the 1950s, documentary photography is showcased and championed. The sheer depth and variety of the visuals add another dimension to the writing, and undiscovered writers are published alongside Nobel Prize winners. A world view where quality ideas matter is the philosophy that underpins the publication.

A new business model for publishing, **tank** relies less on advertising and more on the commitment and support of its readers. Many people don't want to plough through 150 pages of advertising before coming across any feature content. This new economy of scale has given birth to 'boutique publishing'. Within its first year, **tank** achieved a major international following and an unprecedented sell-out success. In turn, its format as a pocket-size 'bookzine' has influenced a generation of magazines, including some in mainstream publishing. **tank** has proven more revolutionary than its collaborators ever imagined. Sweet dreams are made of this.

Malu Halasa

From Editor's Diary, September 1998

Got up.

Thought about making
a magazine named '*TONK*'.

Made magazine.

Had dinner.

Printed magazine.

Disastrous printing error.

Went to bed crying.

contents

destination now.

issue 1, September 1998, cover photo by Justine

an hong

龟头红肿
梅毒花蕾
前列腺炎
尿痛尿难
白带恶臭
软硬下疳
陽萎早
阳萎不举
坚而不久
早
射

流脓
梅毒花
湿疣
前列腺
道流脓
尿痛尿
腔炎
白带
阴痒
软硬
尖等
泄
阳
举而不坚
坚
无精不育
Kiss

masoud

page 13: make-up: Sophia Lewandrowski
page 14: make-up: Charlotte Day
page 15: make-up: Liz Daxauer
models: Chrissy @ IMG · Stacy @ Models 1 · Jamie Gong @ Take 2

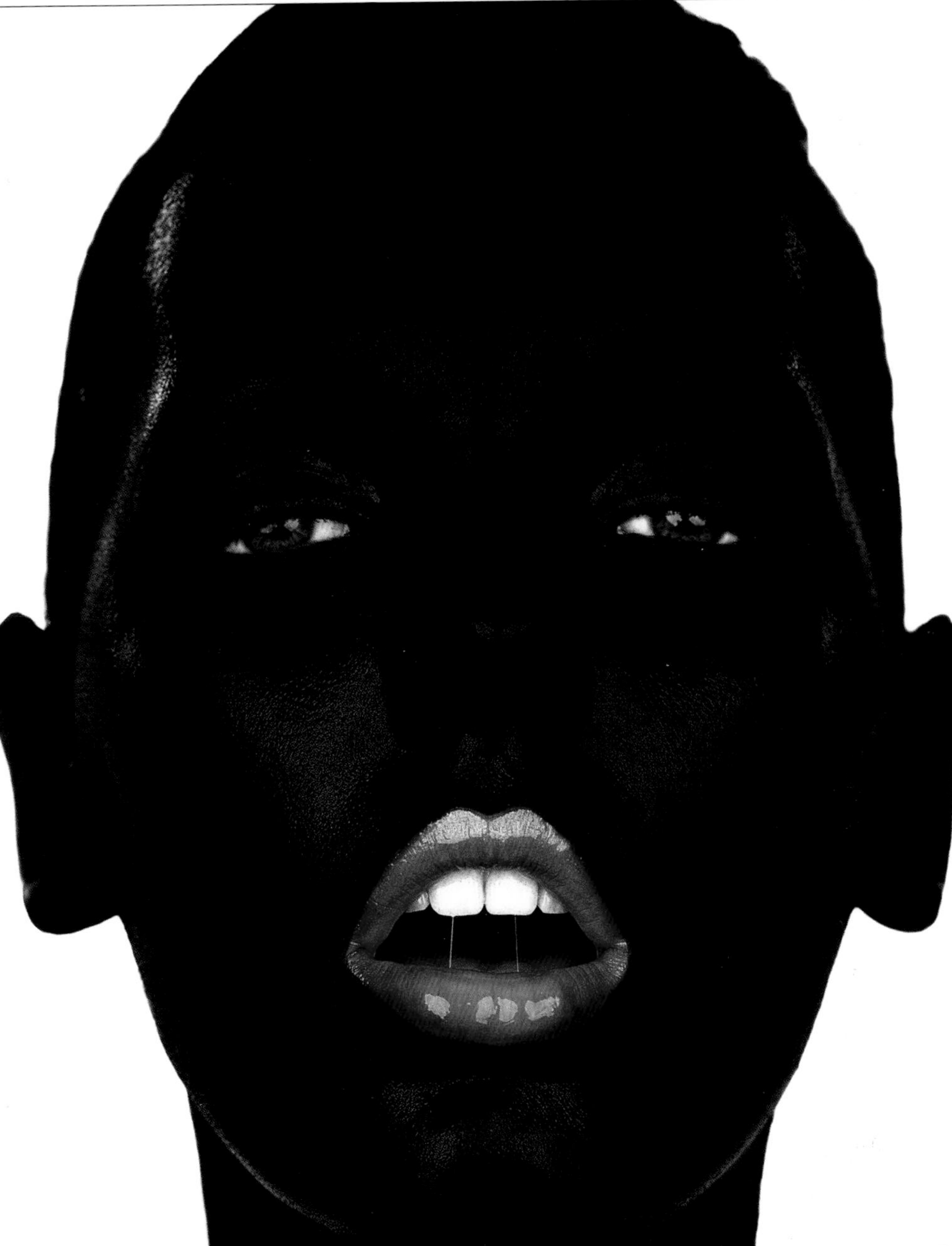

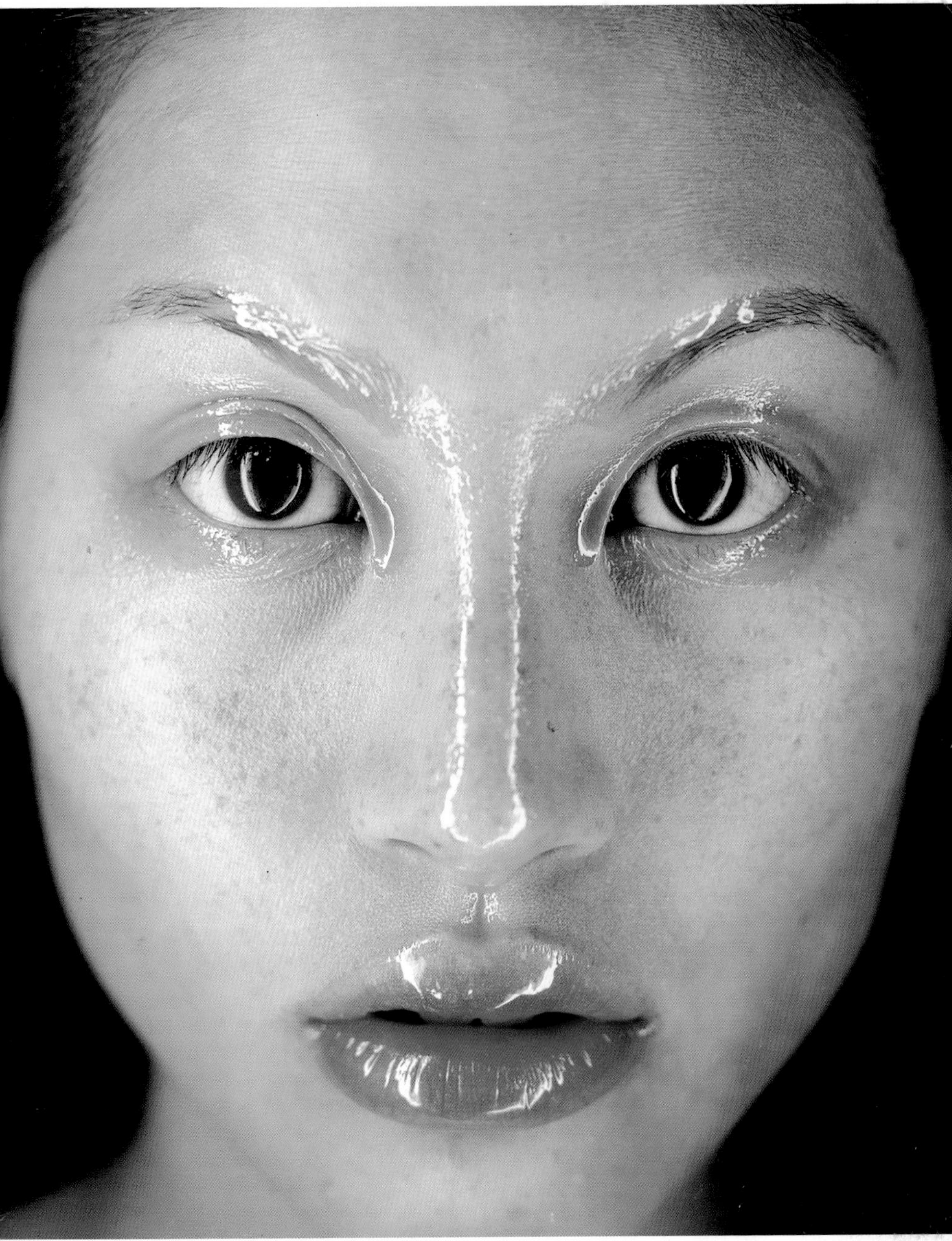

paul
morrison

@ asprey jacques Gallery, London

faster,
better,
harder.

issue 2, December 1998, cover photo by John-Paul Pietrus

barnaby+ scott

styling: Geriada Kefford
hair: Jennie Roberts

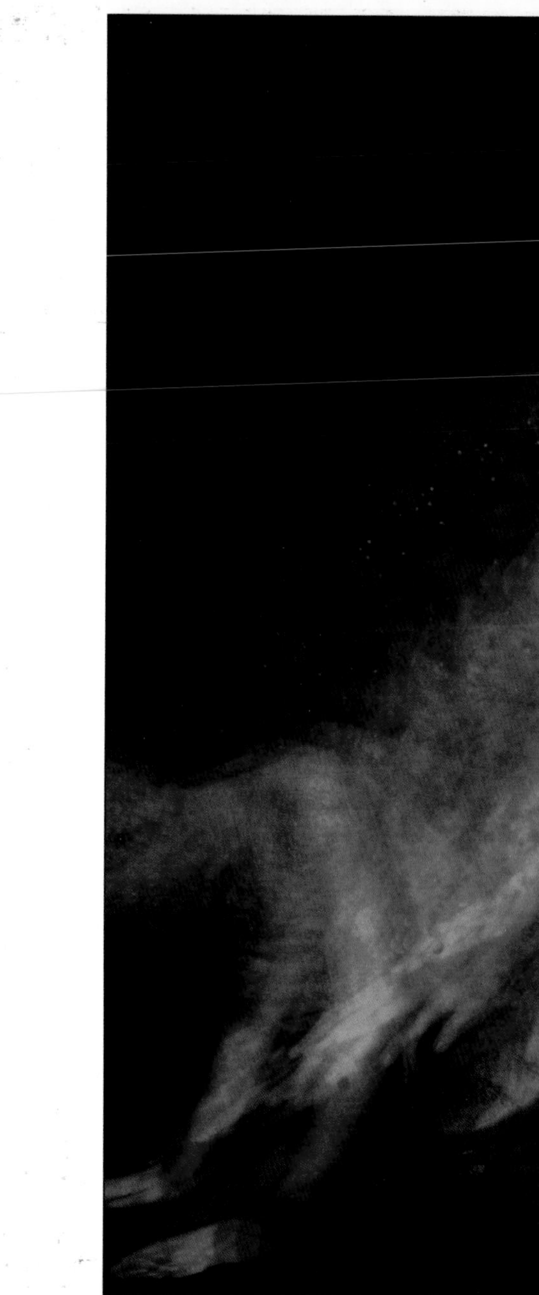

bump

FAT-
SLAG

SIL-
ENCE

nO -
IdEA

run-
riot

john-paul pietrus

styling: Jo Phillips
hair: Jeannie Roberts
make-up: J. Maskery
model: Eva Strus @ Two Management

laura
sciacovelli

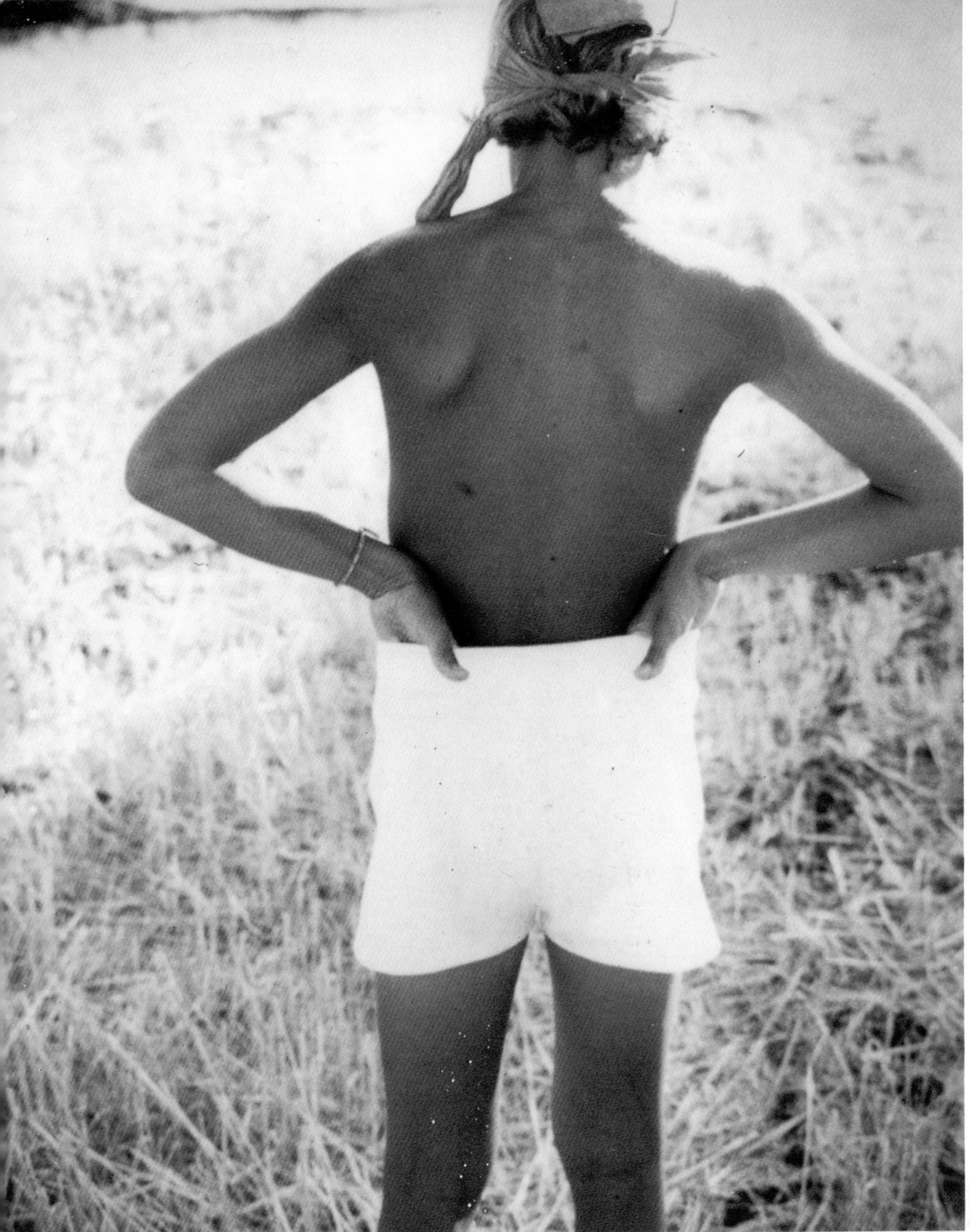

kai wiechmann

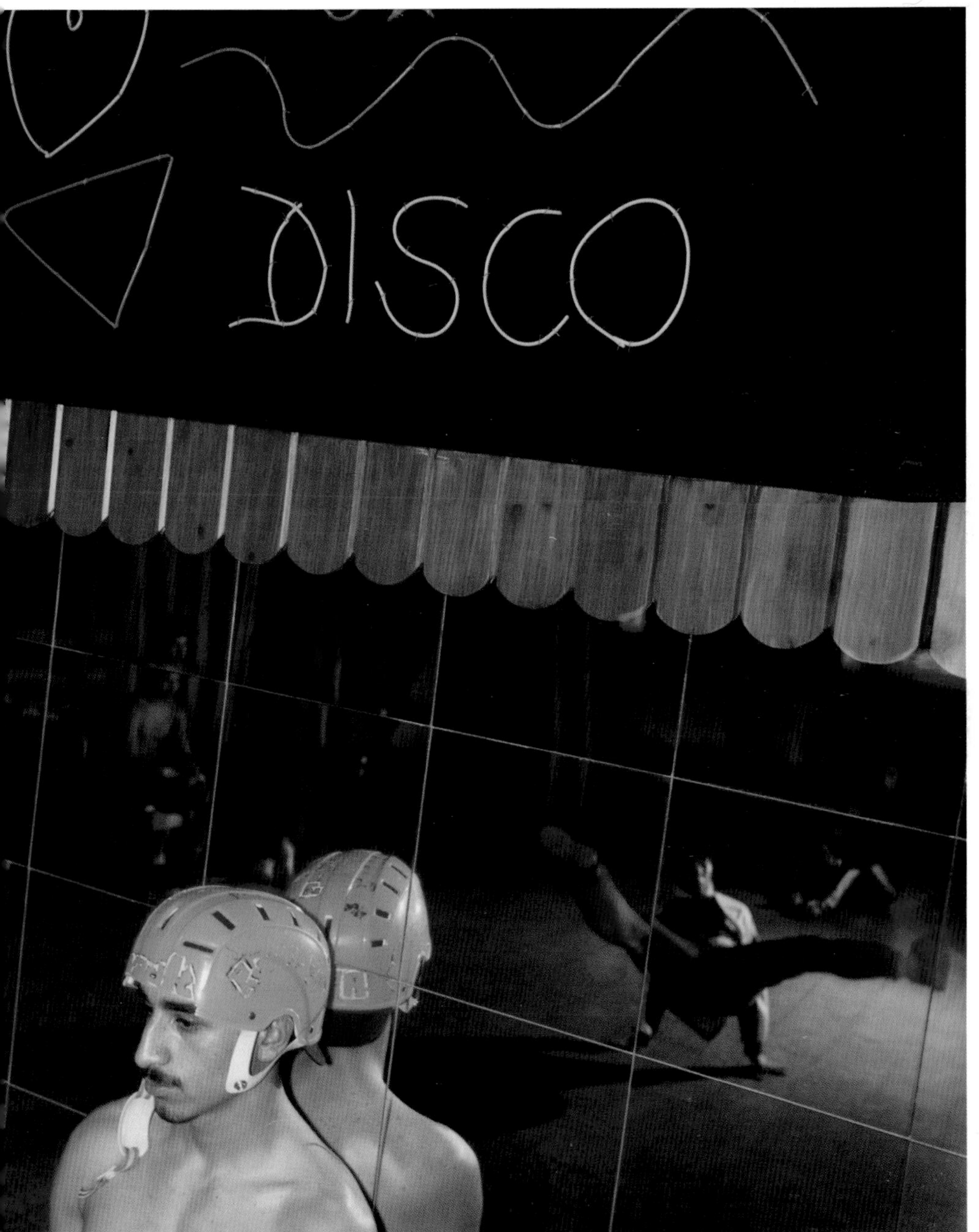
DISCO

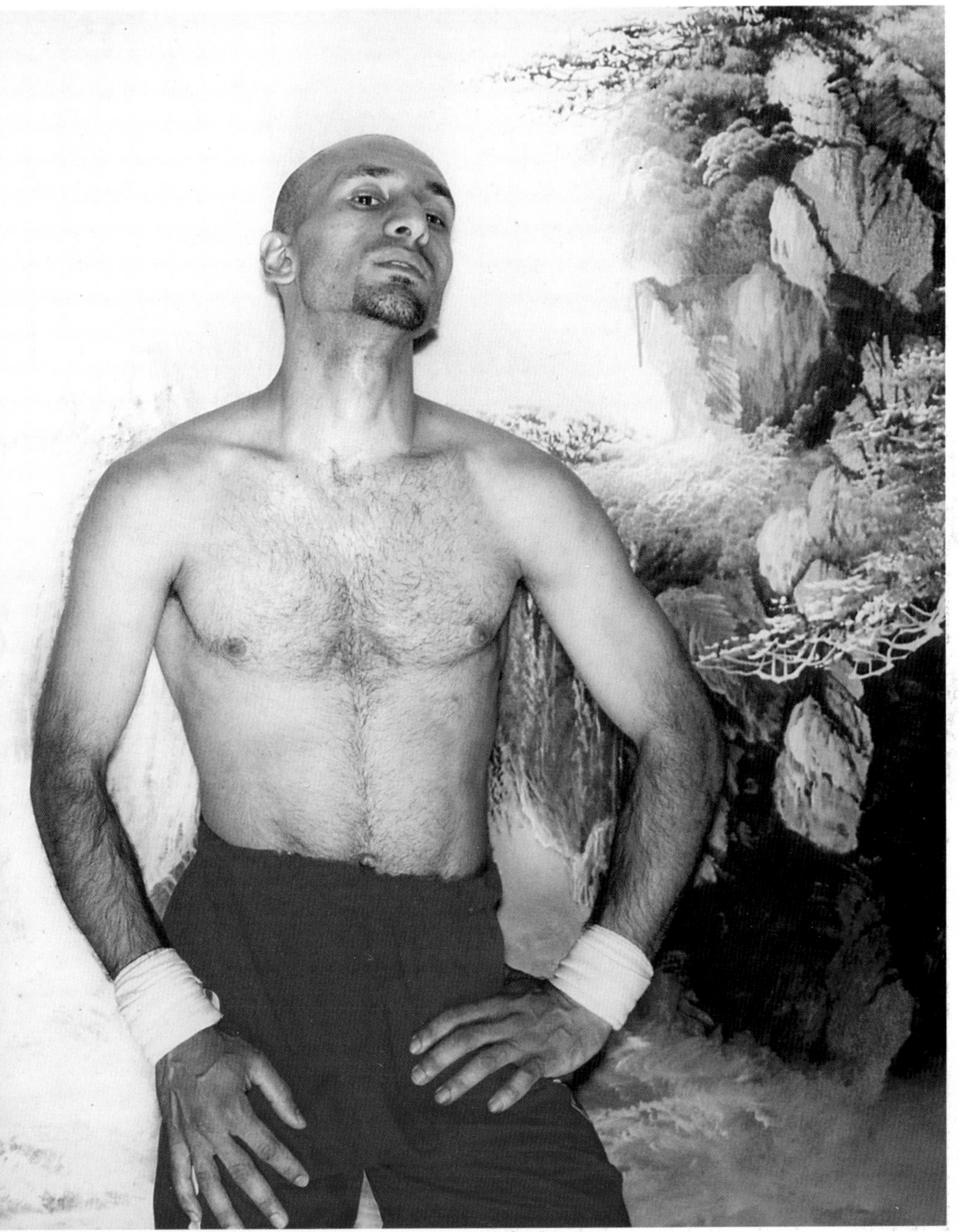

peter garfield

courtesy Feigen Gallery + VAGA, New York

1

tım brett day

styling: Alison Fitzpatrick
make-up: Aimee Adams
hair: Matthew Cross
models: Lucia + Maddie @ Premier

sean mellyn

courtesy Anna Kustera Gallery, New York

December 1998

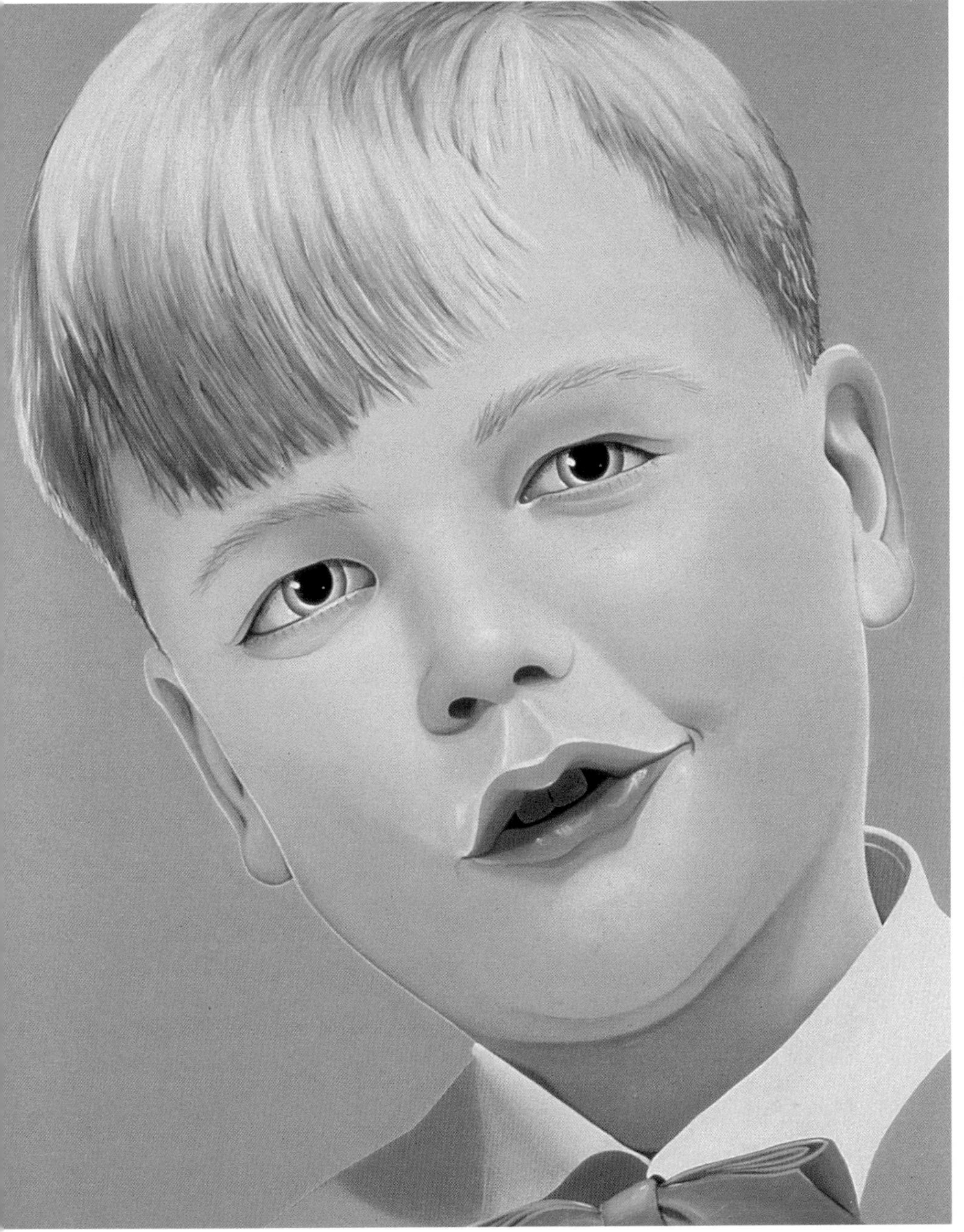

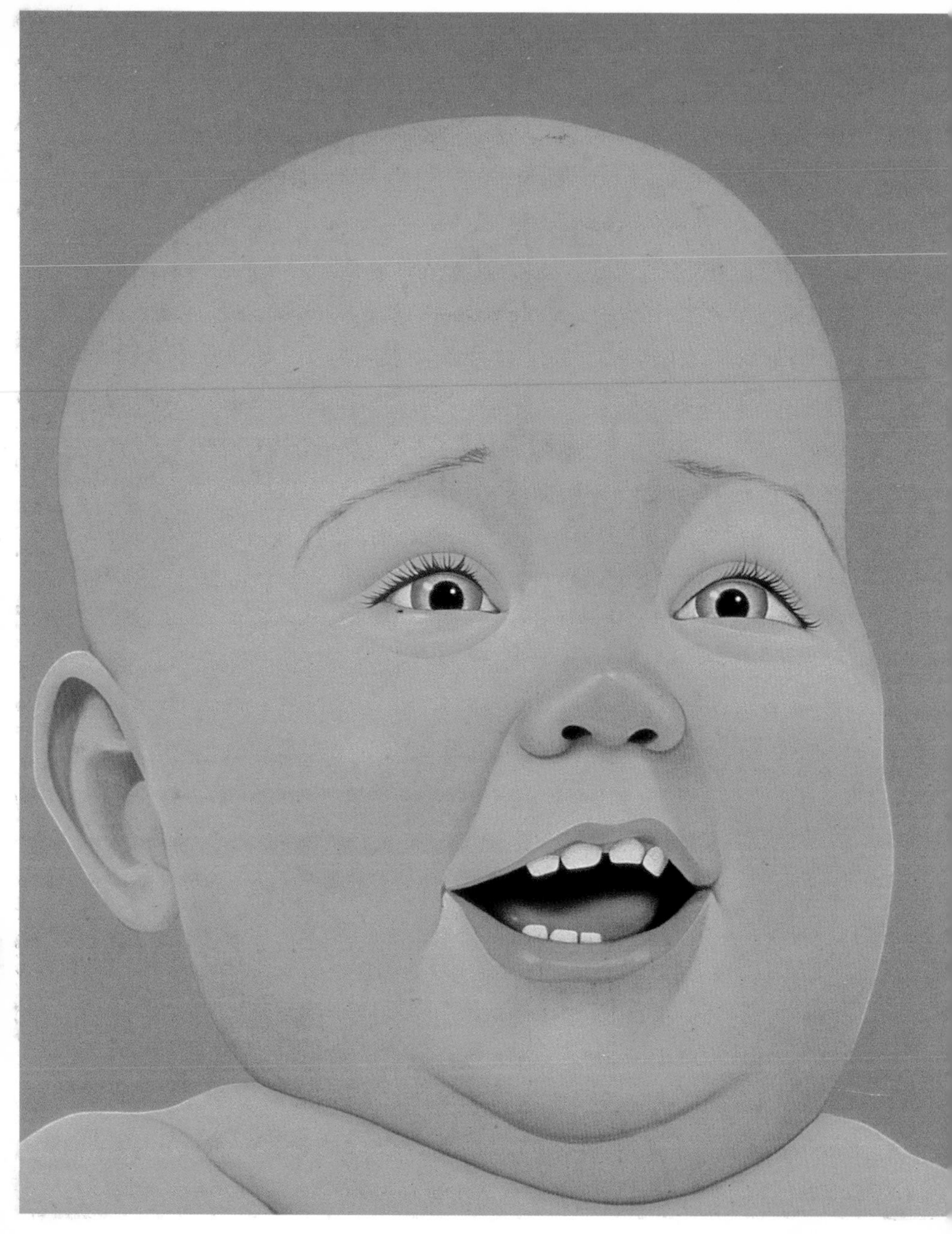

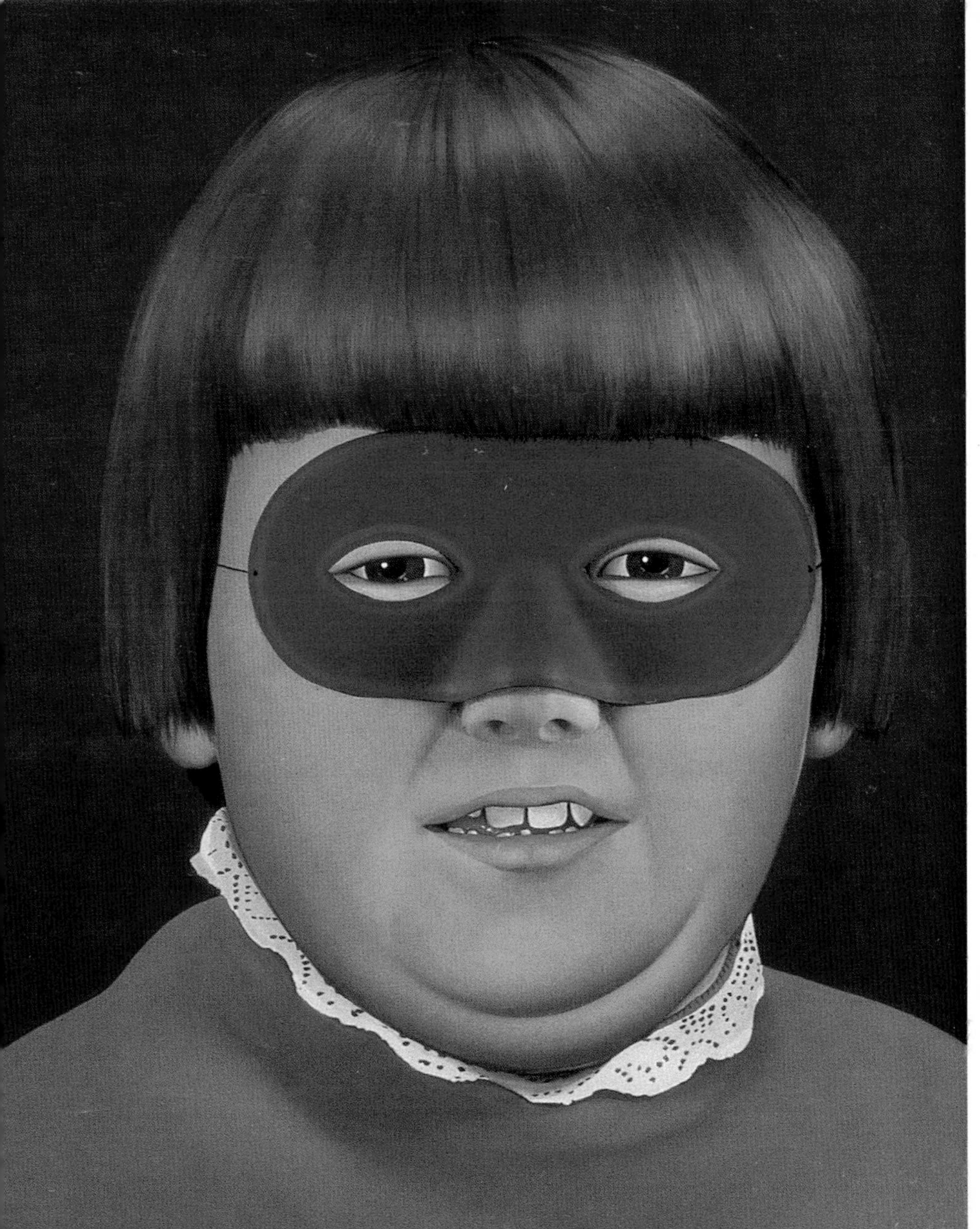

jonathan west

styling: Maria Serra
hair: Moose
make-up: Angela Cheung
models: Nancy Hagaan + Susanne Crozier @ Select

December 1998

Iko ouro preto

fred tomaselli

courtesy Jack Tilton Gallery, New York

donovan wylie

courtesy of Donovan Wylie / Magnum Photos London + 4th Estate, London

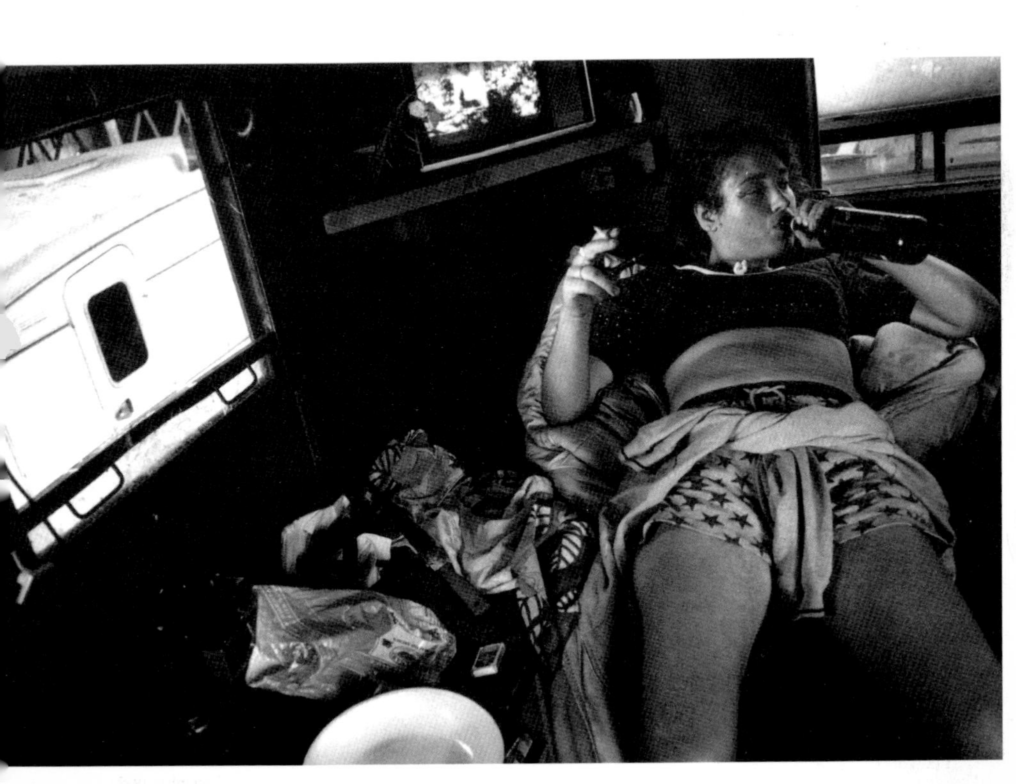

ULSTER
SOUTH BELFAST...
UNCLE TONY...
TWOSA
McCANN
CHAOS
I DON'T GIVE A TOSS

MOT
PECE

julie verhoeven

December 1998

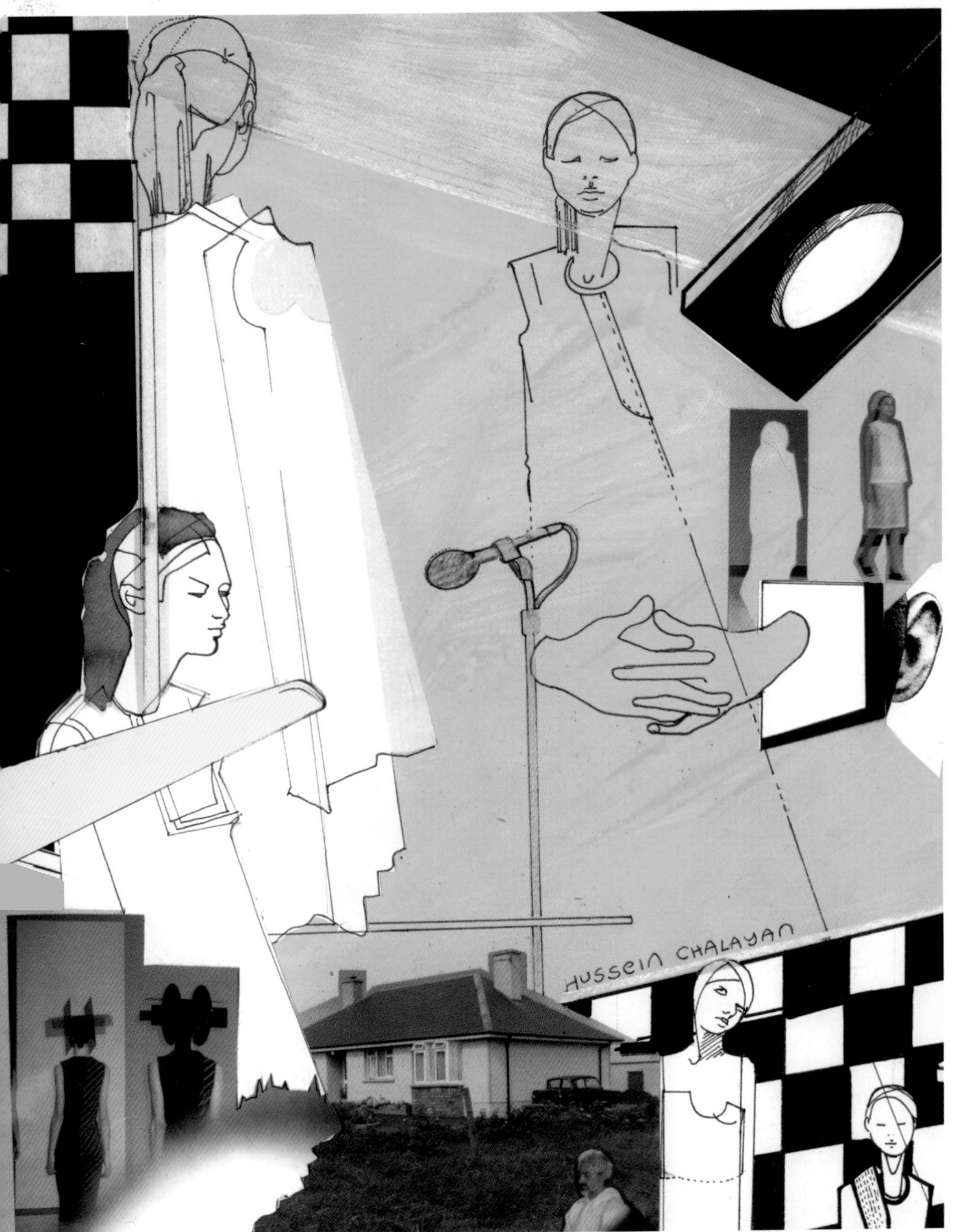
HUSSEIN CHALAYAN

the good book.

issue 3, February 1999, cover photo by Masoud

crena watson

hair: Raphael Salley ·
make-up: Glen Jackson
models: Zoe Manzi · Samia Bayou · Katy Lyons @ Models 1
Rebeka Bardou @ Premier

February 1999

gottfried helnwein

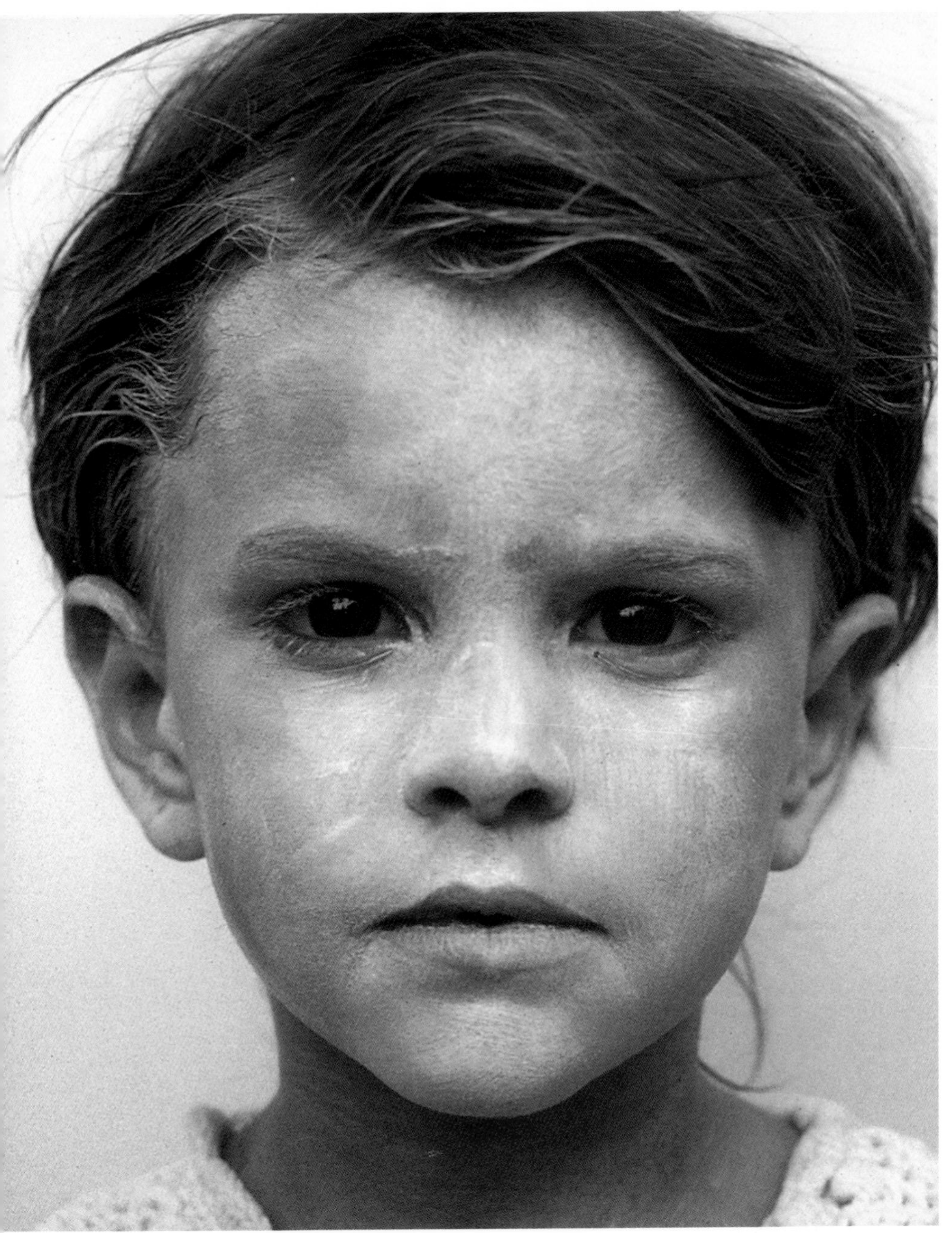

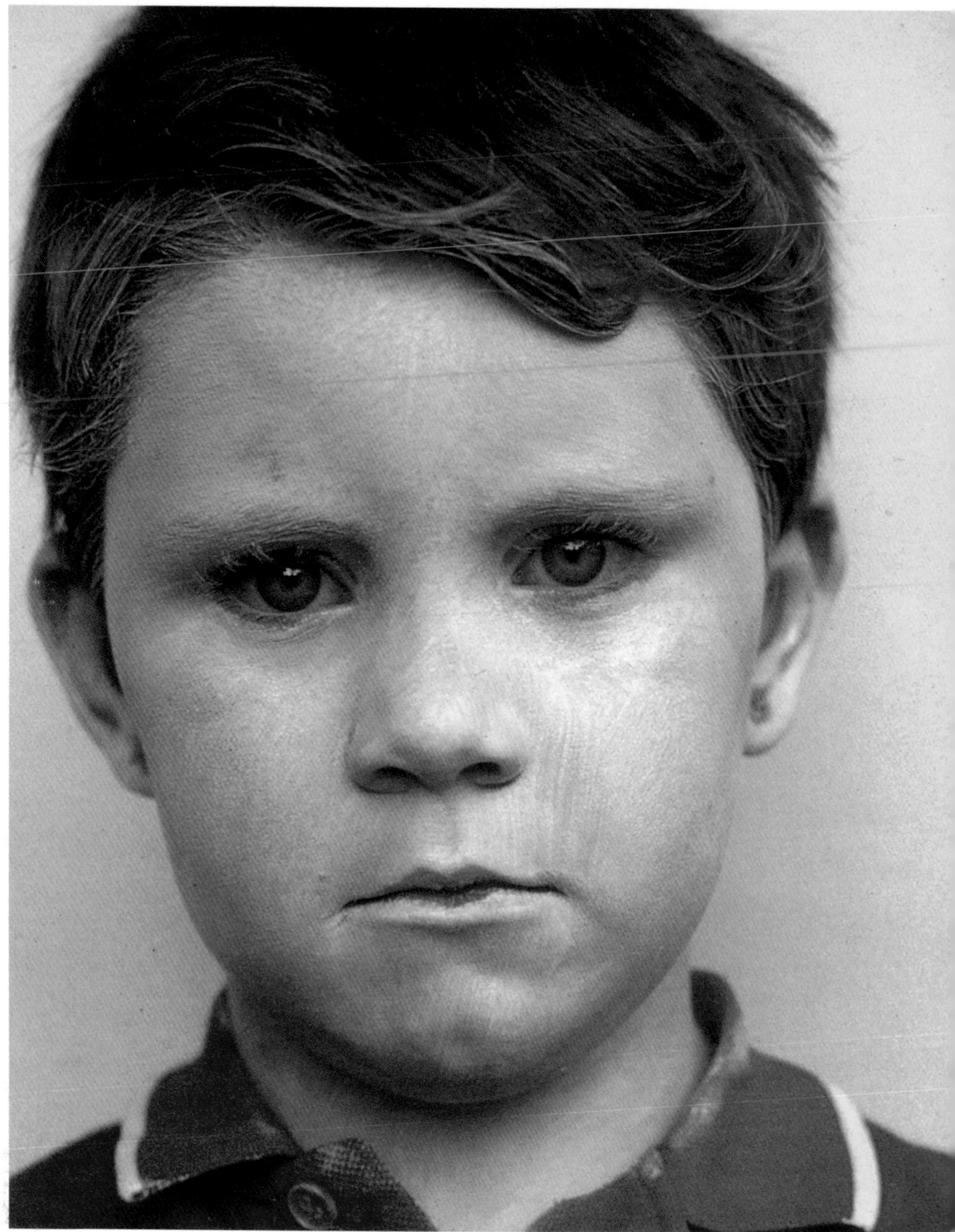

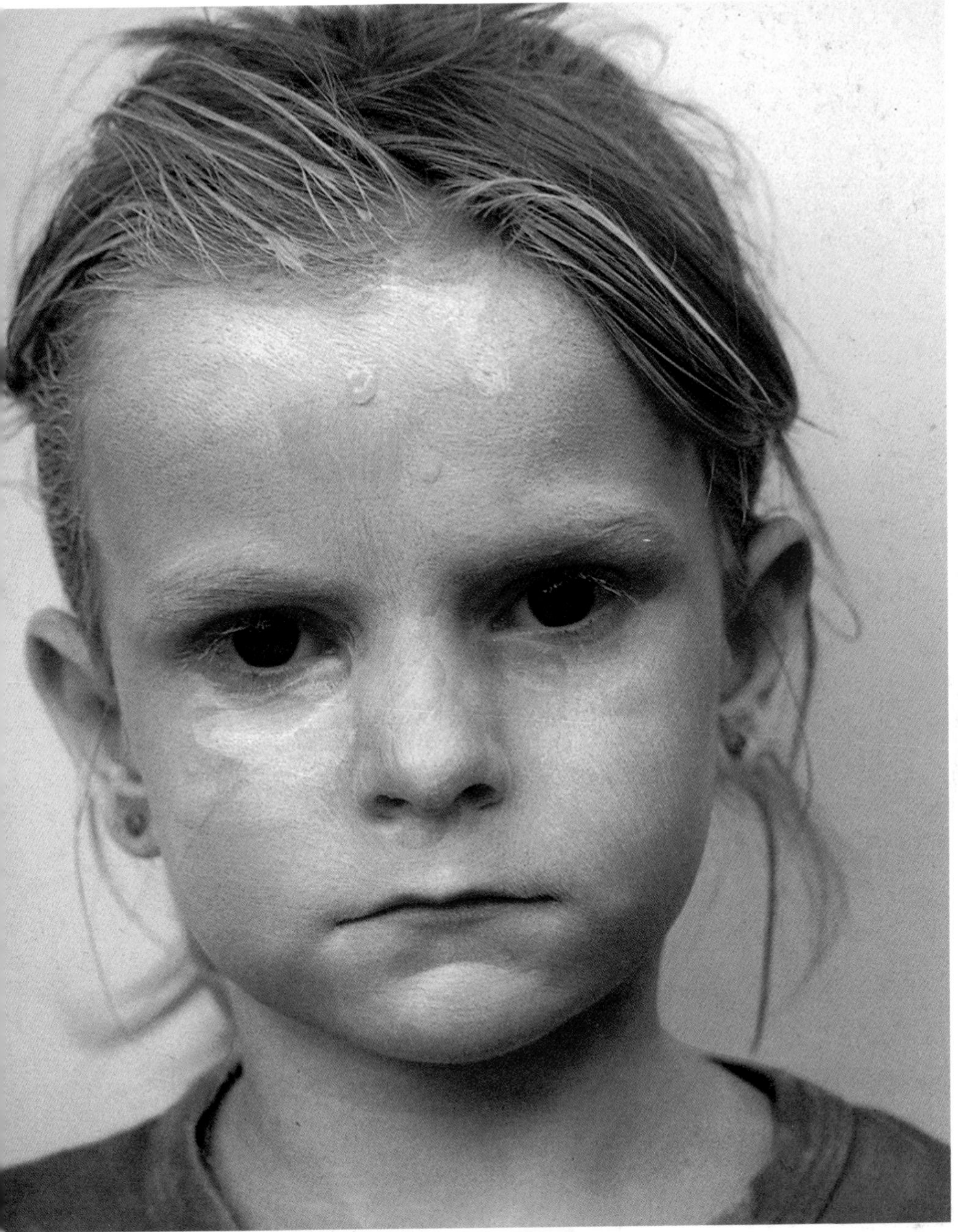

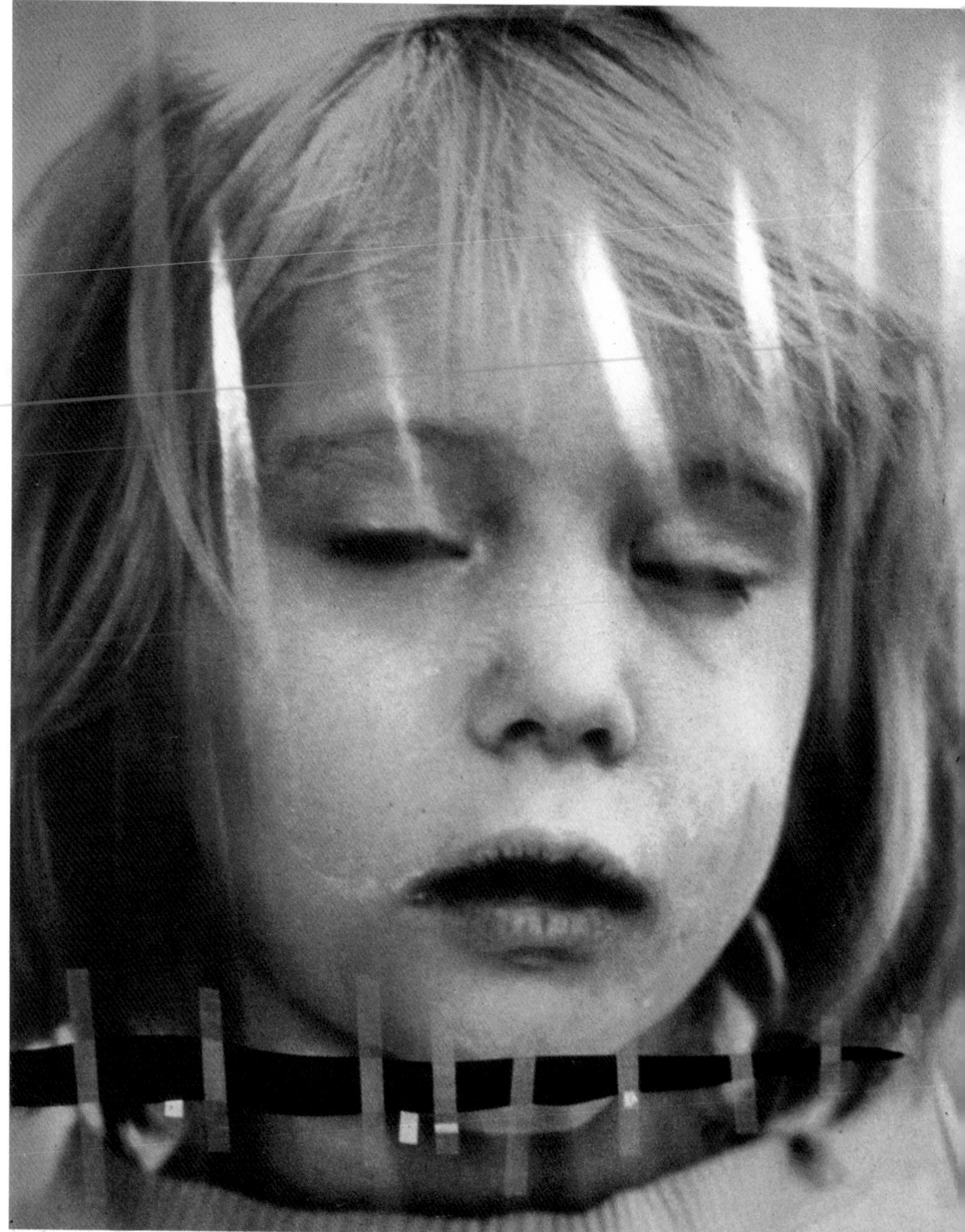

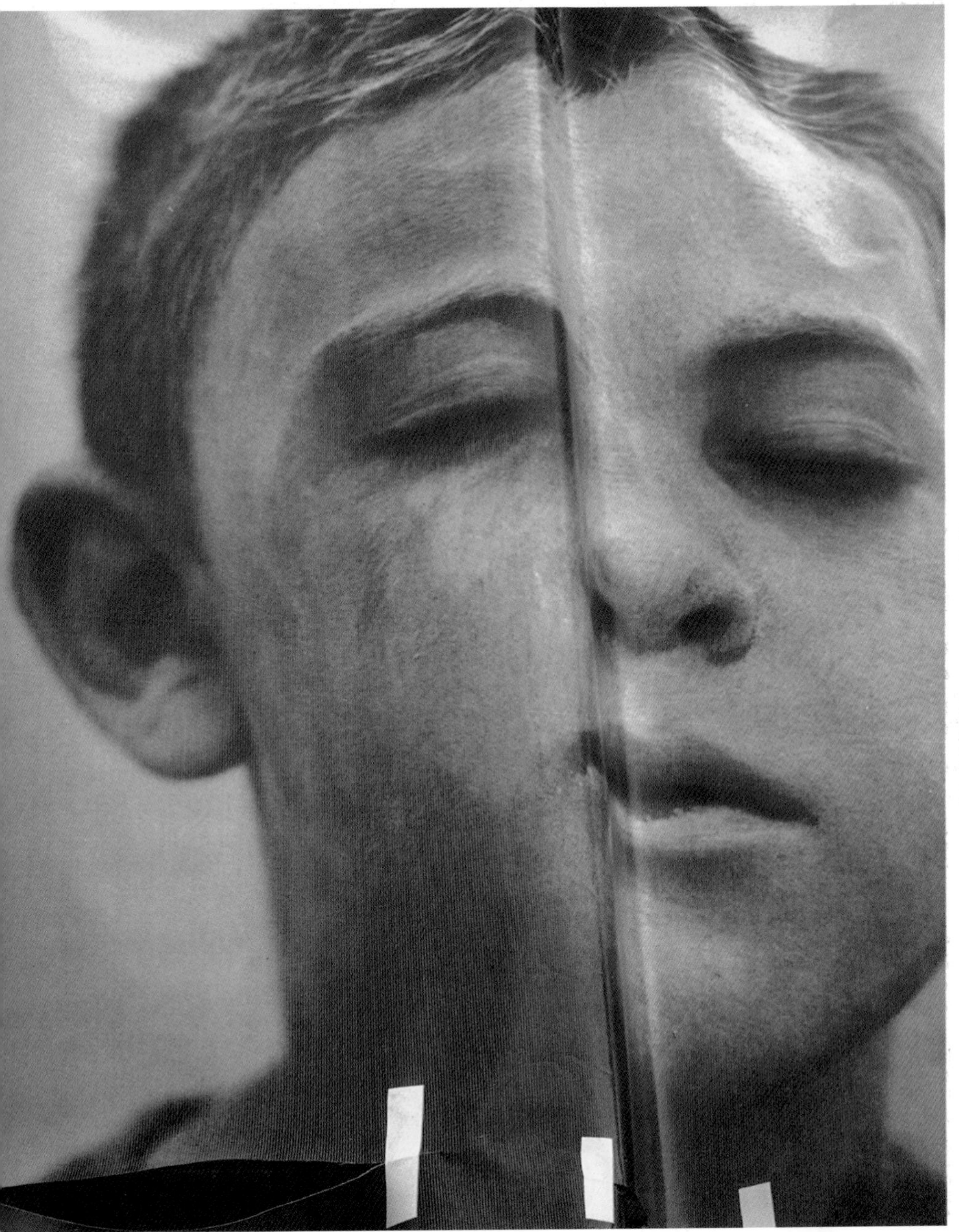

david gibson

February 1999

TRANSFERS
ADDITIONAL
LADIES &
GENTLEMEN

ALL STOCK
GREATLY
REDUCED

fabio almeida

with the help of Adrian Self

February 1999

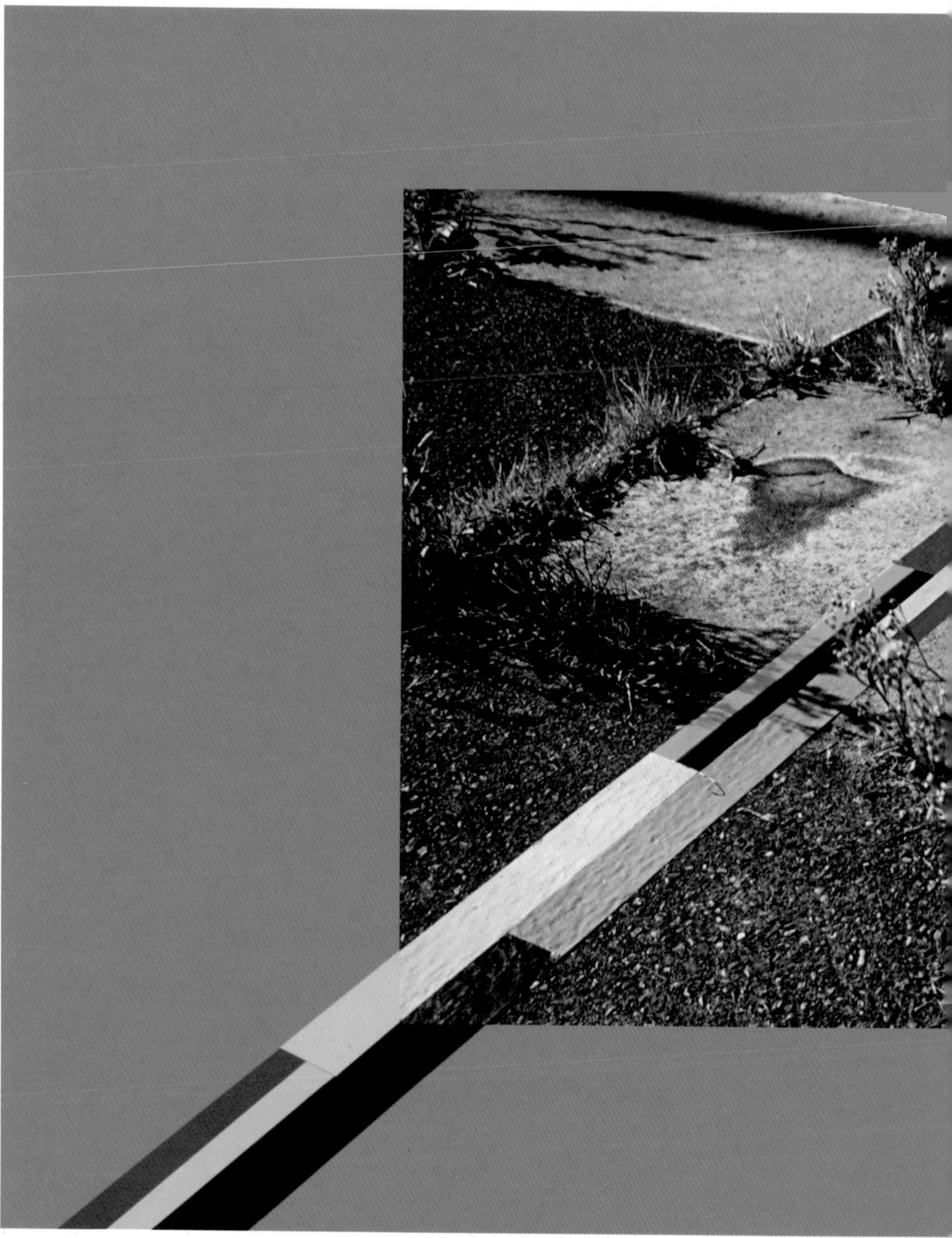

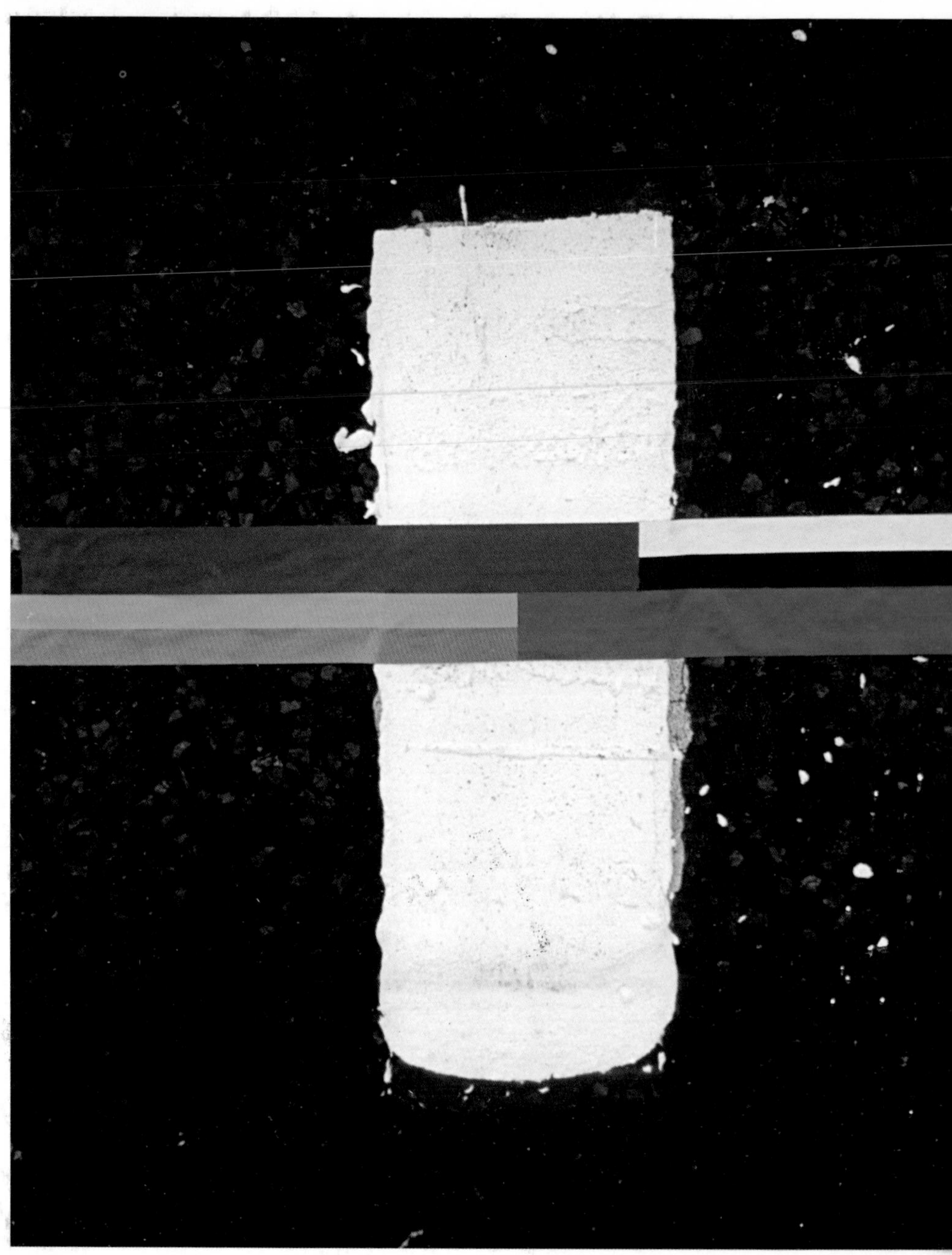

gregory crewdson

@ Emily Tsingou Gallery, London
courtesy Luhring Augustine, New York

February 1999

matthieu deluc

styling: Christophe Martinez
hair: Fouad + Katherine Verxeman
make-up: Marmotte
model: Melissa Peters @ Metropolitan + Juliette

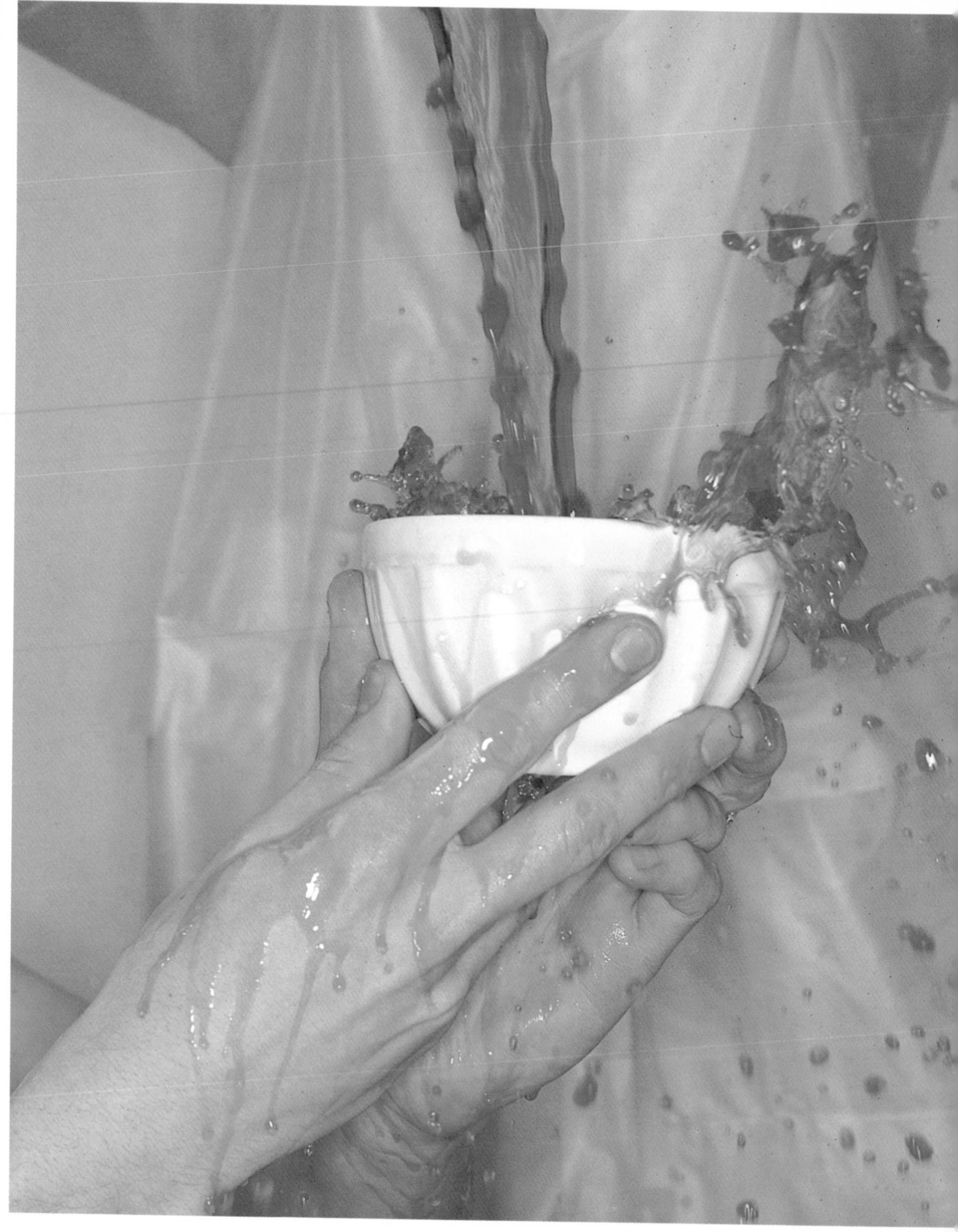

Dior
CHANEL
GIVENCHY

slıppeye

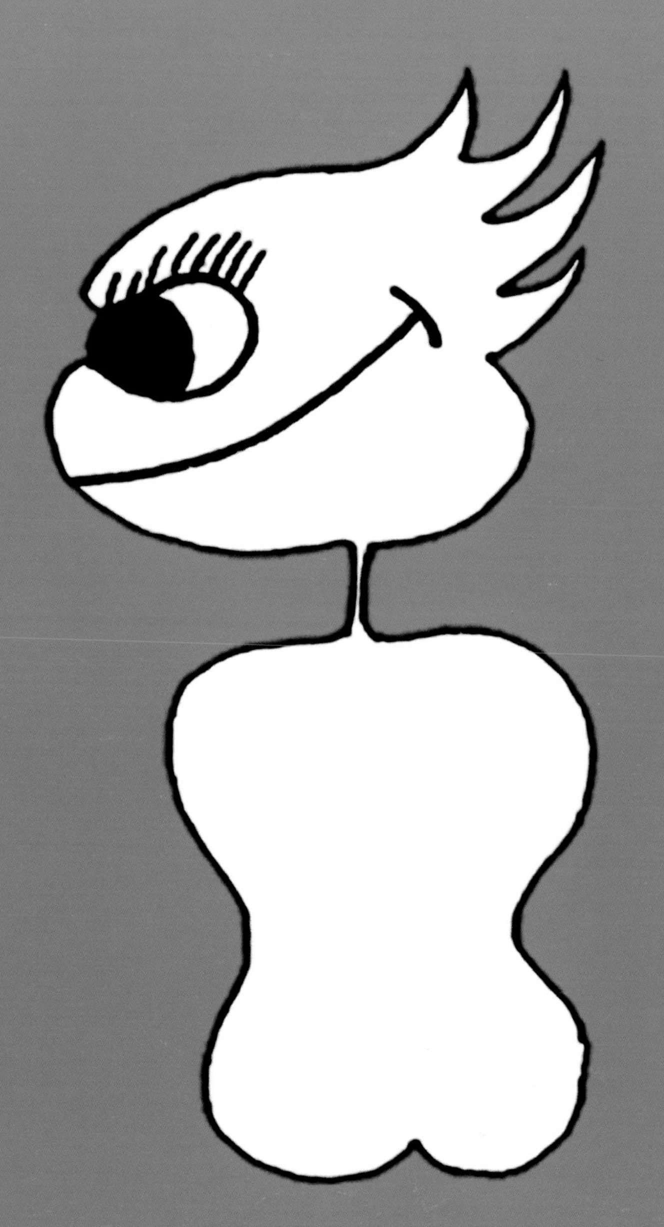

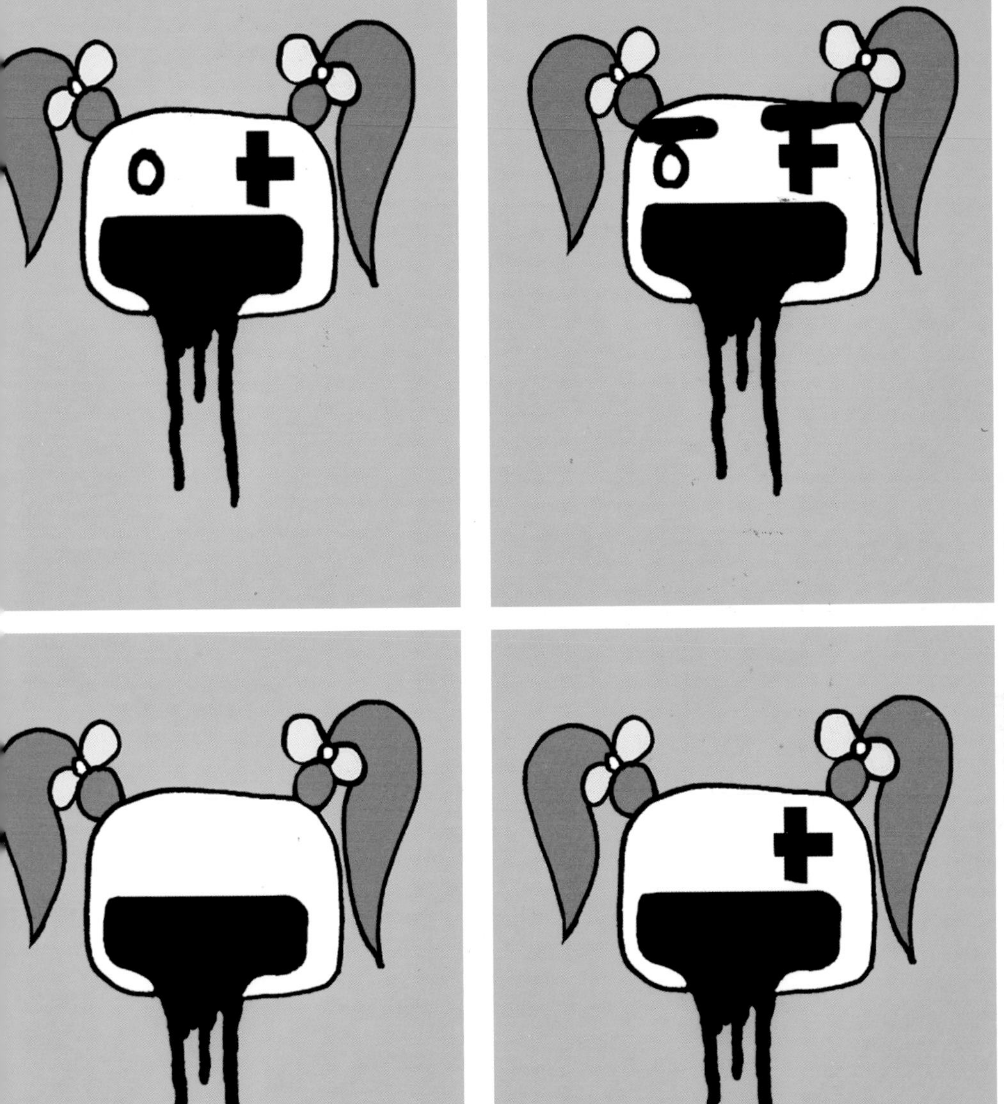

txema yeste

VITALICIO

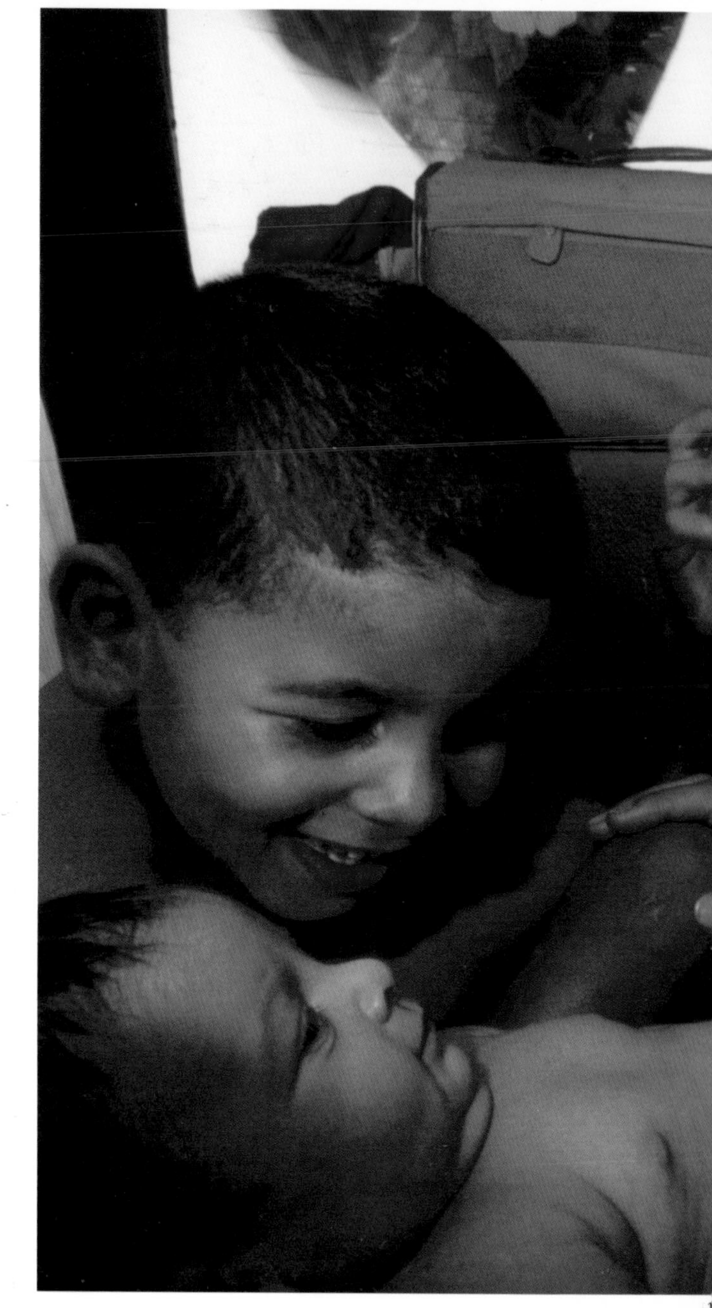

courtesy of Magnum Photos London

برقرار با
ضد امپریالیستی و دمکراتیک ایران در
حزب توده ایران

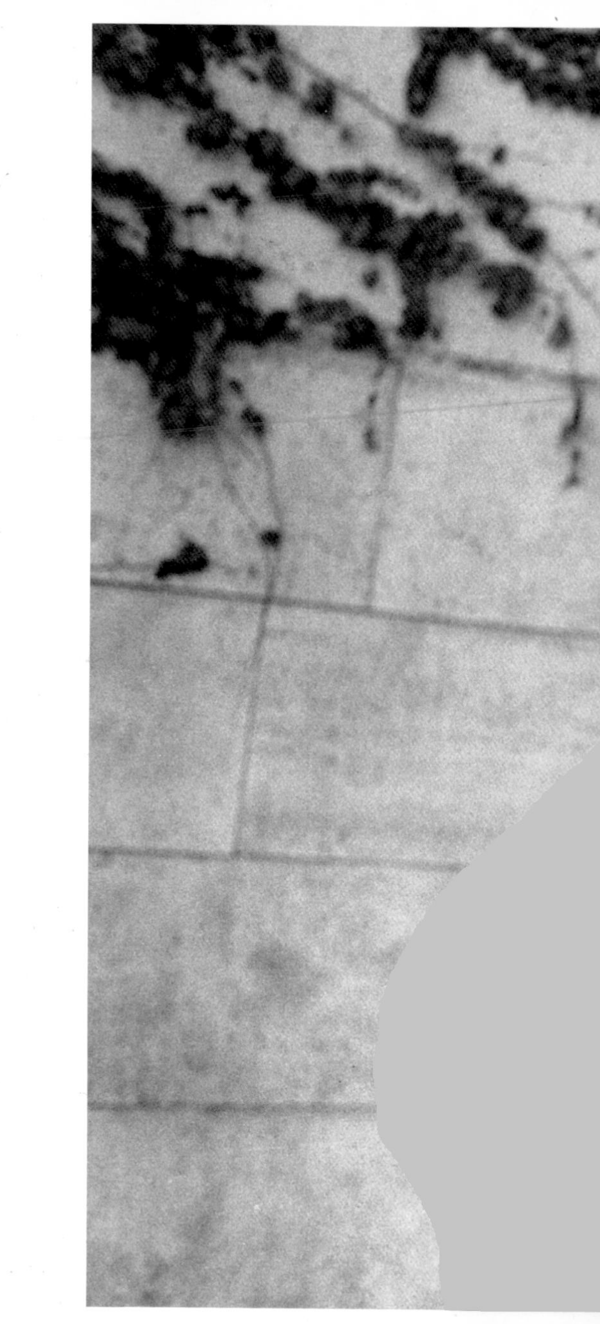

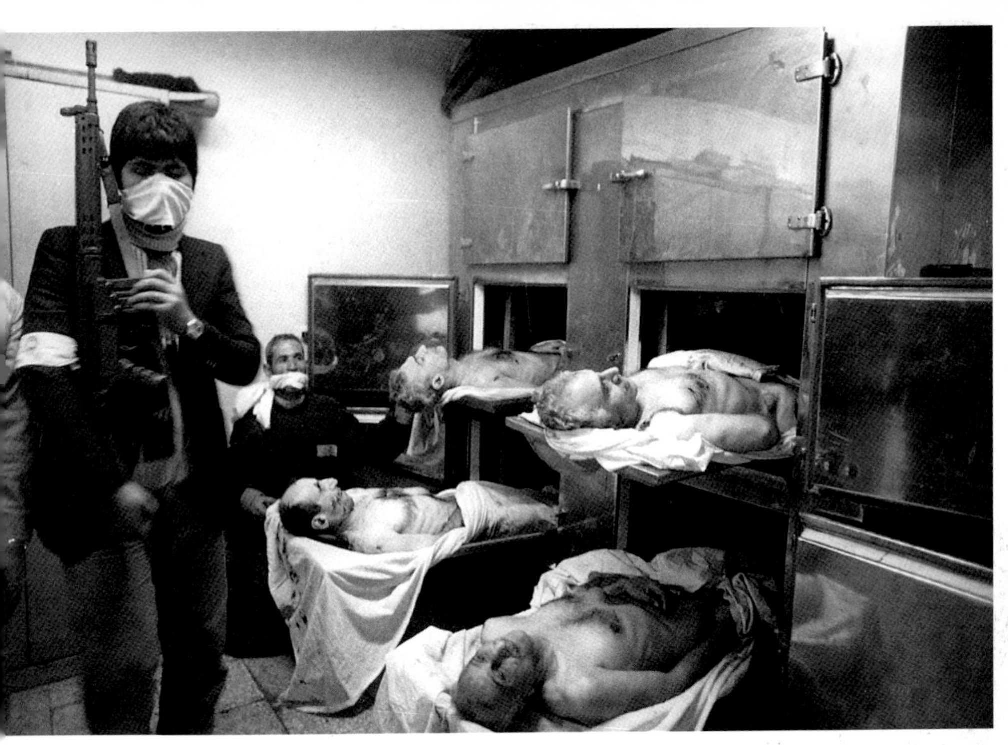

pale into significance.

issue 4, April 1999, cover photo by Alessandro Dal Buoni

barnaby+ scott

styling: Charty Durrant
hair: Mandy Lyons
make-up: Debbie Stone
dancers: Ruth Lloyd + Litza Bixlier

carter kustera

courtesy Anna Kustera Gallery, New York

CALVIN

USES A PSYCHIC TO PICK HIS LOTTERY NUMBERS

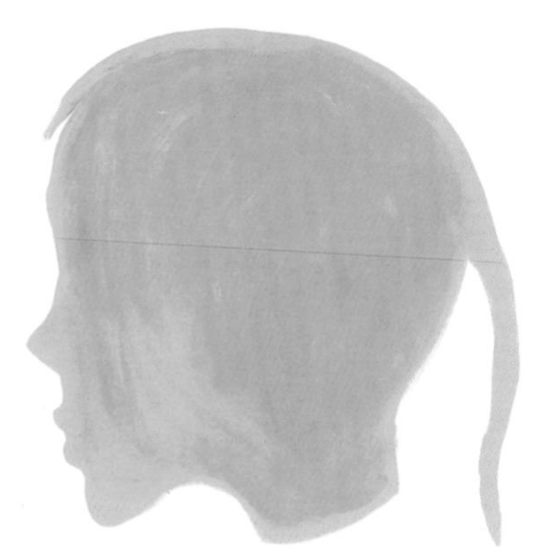

PATRICIA

SAY'S HER MOM REFUSES TO GROW UP

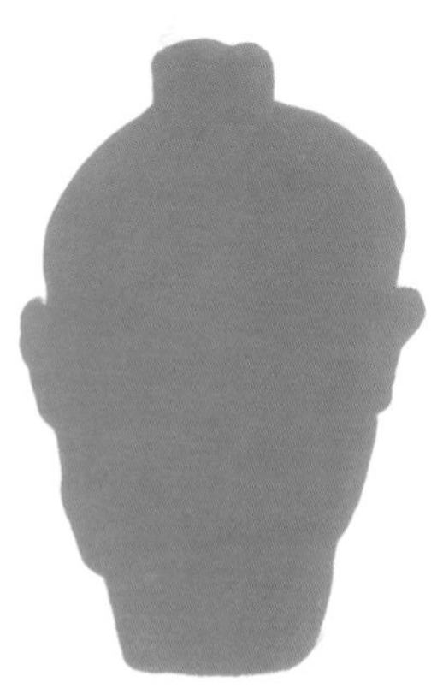

LOTHER

NOT READY FOR THE COMPUTER AGE

MICKY

SAY'S HIS GIRLFRIEND DRIVES HIM CRAZY

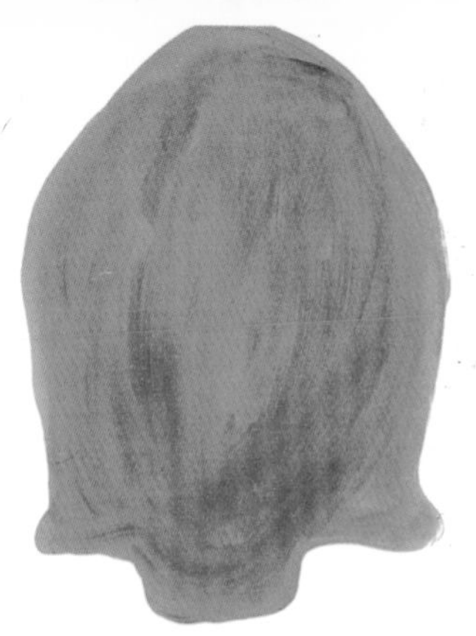

MEAGAN

MARRIED TO TWO MEN AT THE SAME TIME

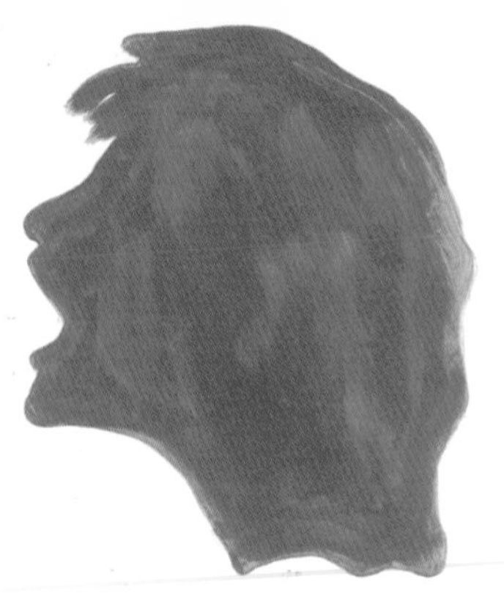

JESSICA

WAS ADOPTED AS AN INFANT

BILL

BUY AMERICAN, BUY AMERICAN, BUY AMERICAN

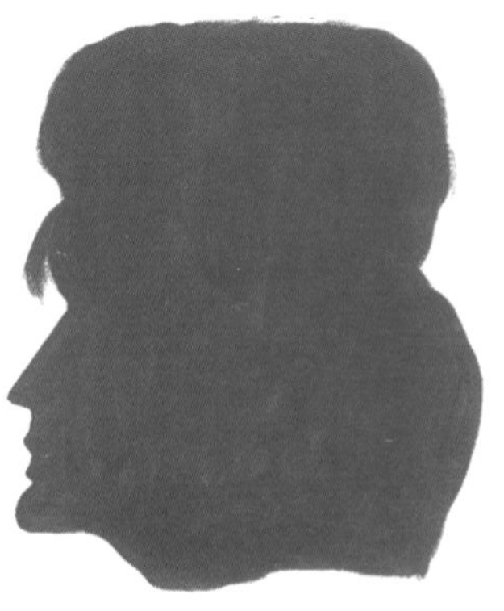

MYRA

WORKS 60 HOURS A WEEK TO SUPPORT HER ARTIST HUSBAND

BEATRICE

CLAIMS SHE CAN COMMUNICATE WITH THE DEAD

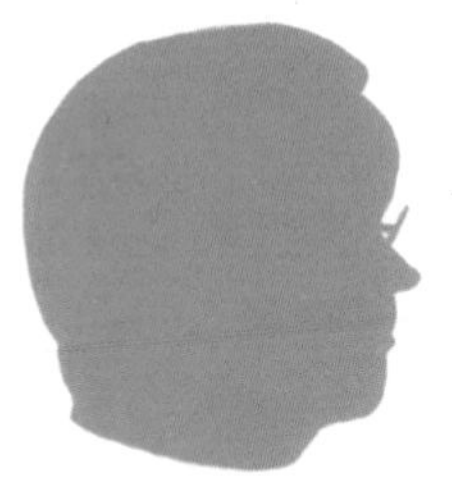

ALFRED
THE ONLY THING HE HATES MORE THAN HIS NAME IS HIS JOB

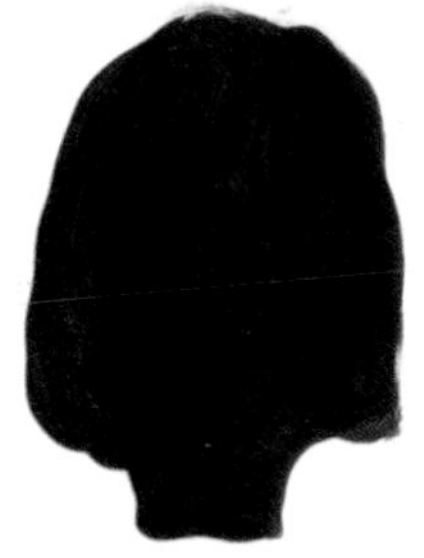

LYNN
WAS MARRIED TO A VIOLENT ALCOHOLIC

MARRY
IS JEALOUS OF HER SISTER

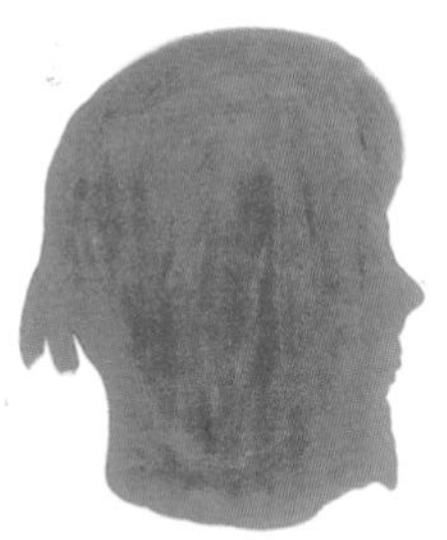

JASON
IS A SPORTS FANATIC

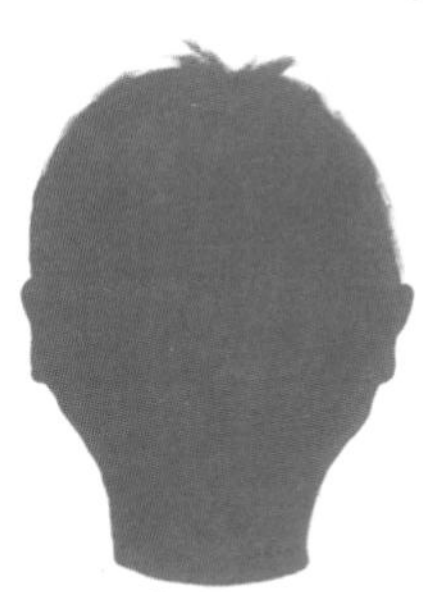

DAN
IN GOD WE TRUST ALL OTHERS PAY CASH

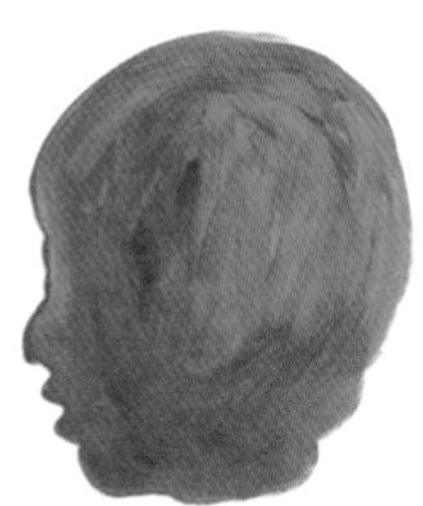

ADAM
WAITING UNTIL MARRIAGE TO HAVE SEX AGAIN

GINA 45,
IS A METAL HEAD

COREY
SAID BEST FRIEND ASKED HIM TO LIE FOR HIM

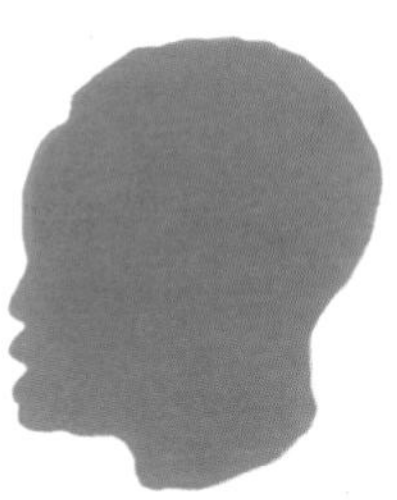

MANNY
THINKS YOU DON'T HAVE TO WEAR A SUIT AND TIE TO BE PROFESSIONAL

chen yuanzhong

April 1999

elaine dugan

April 1999

Bradypus tridactylus
3480

H.124·1

Delphinus.

eric maillet

styling: Rolland Mouret
models: Marieke de Lange @ Fam · Samuel @ Click · Cedric @ Karin

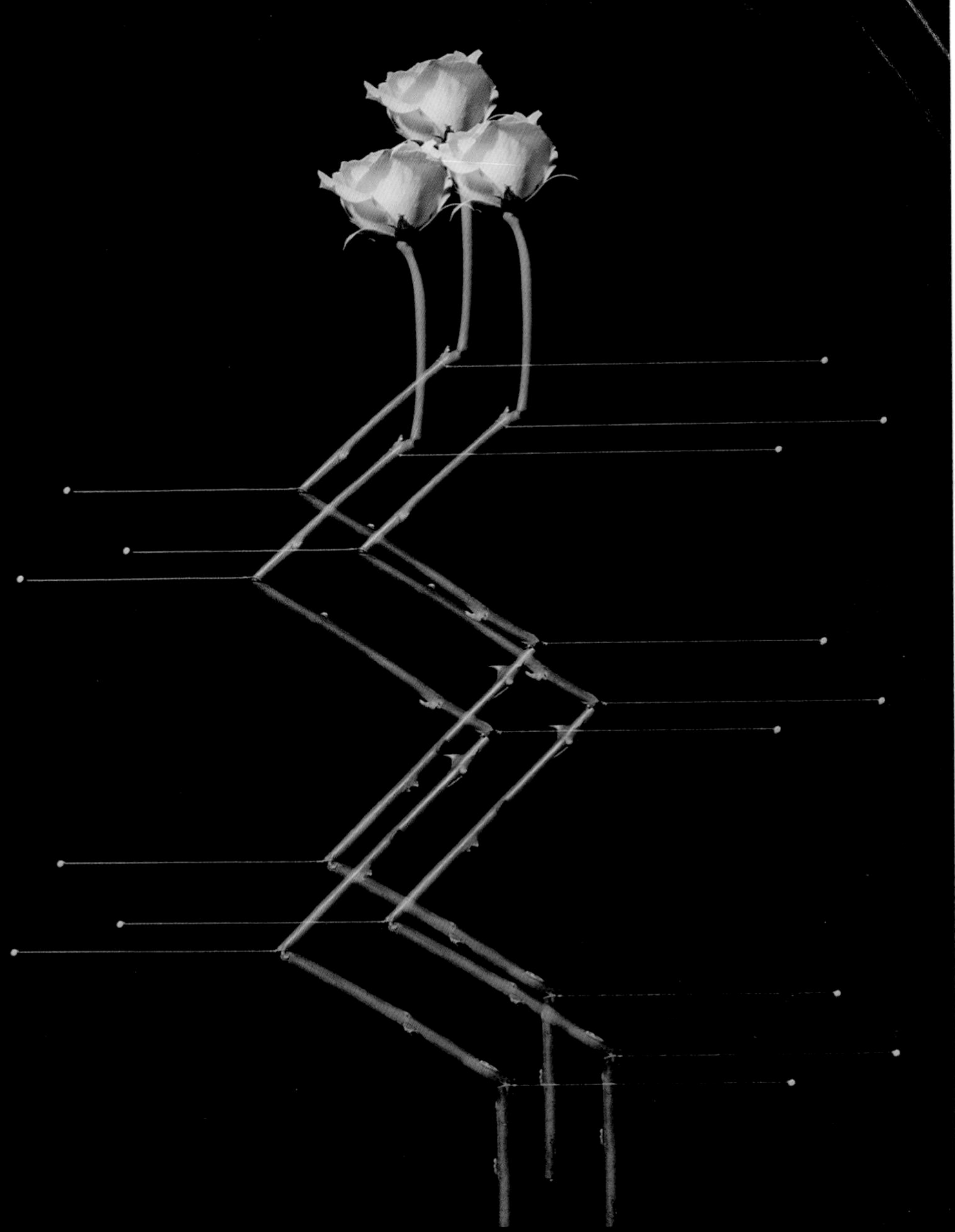

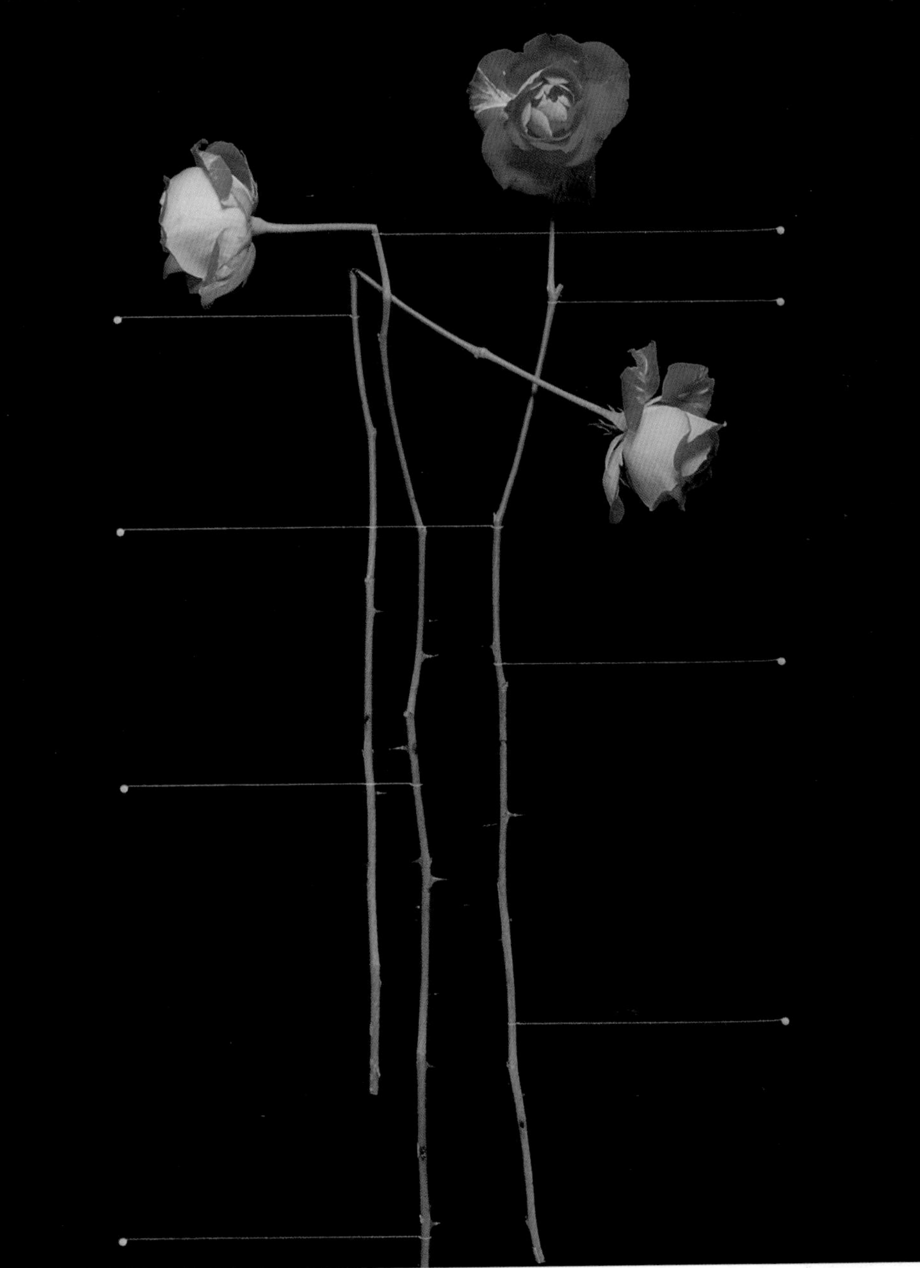

jens boldt

styling: Simone Gampe
hair/make-up: Jerome Guiton

April 1999

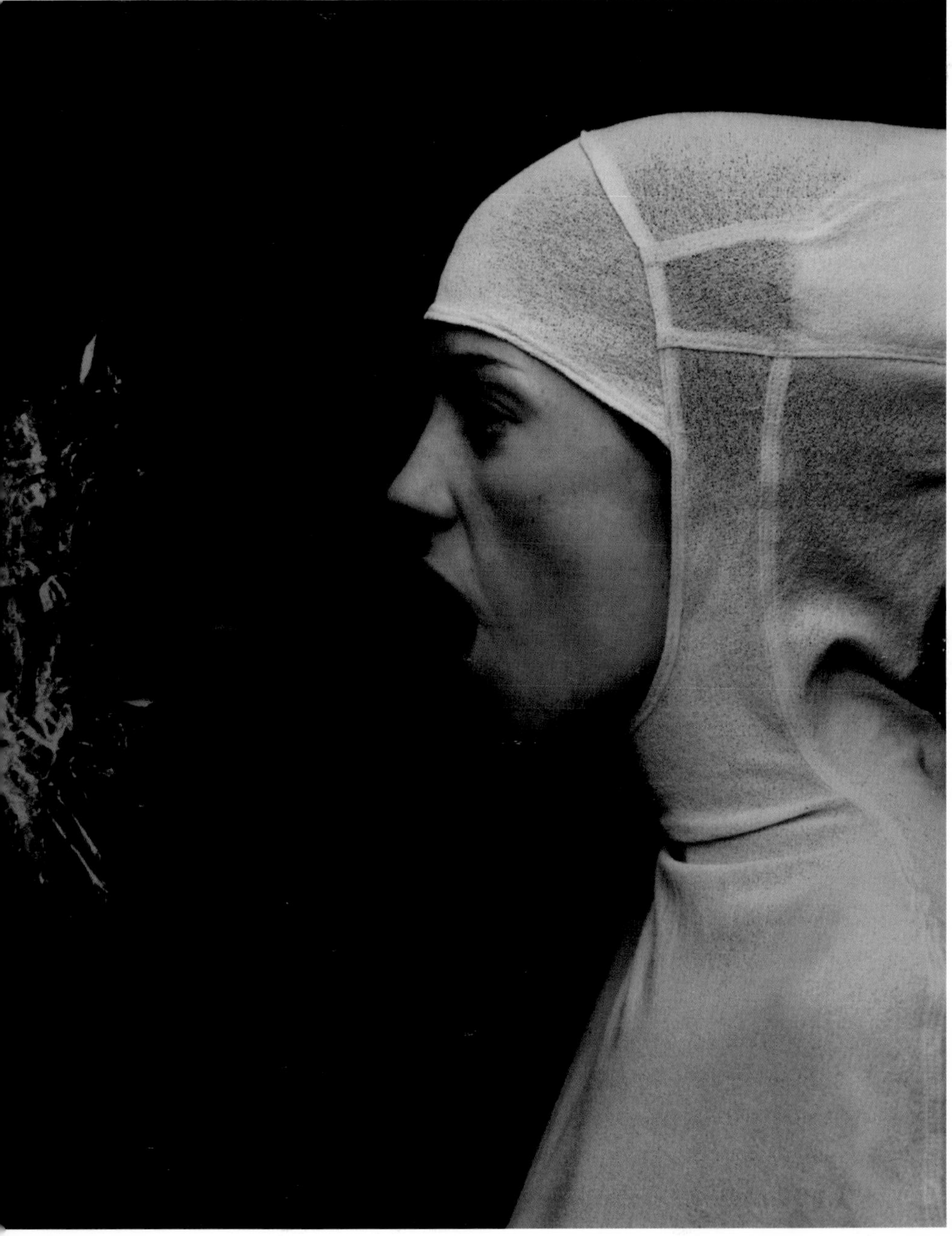

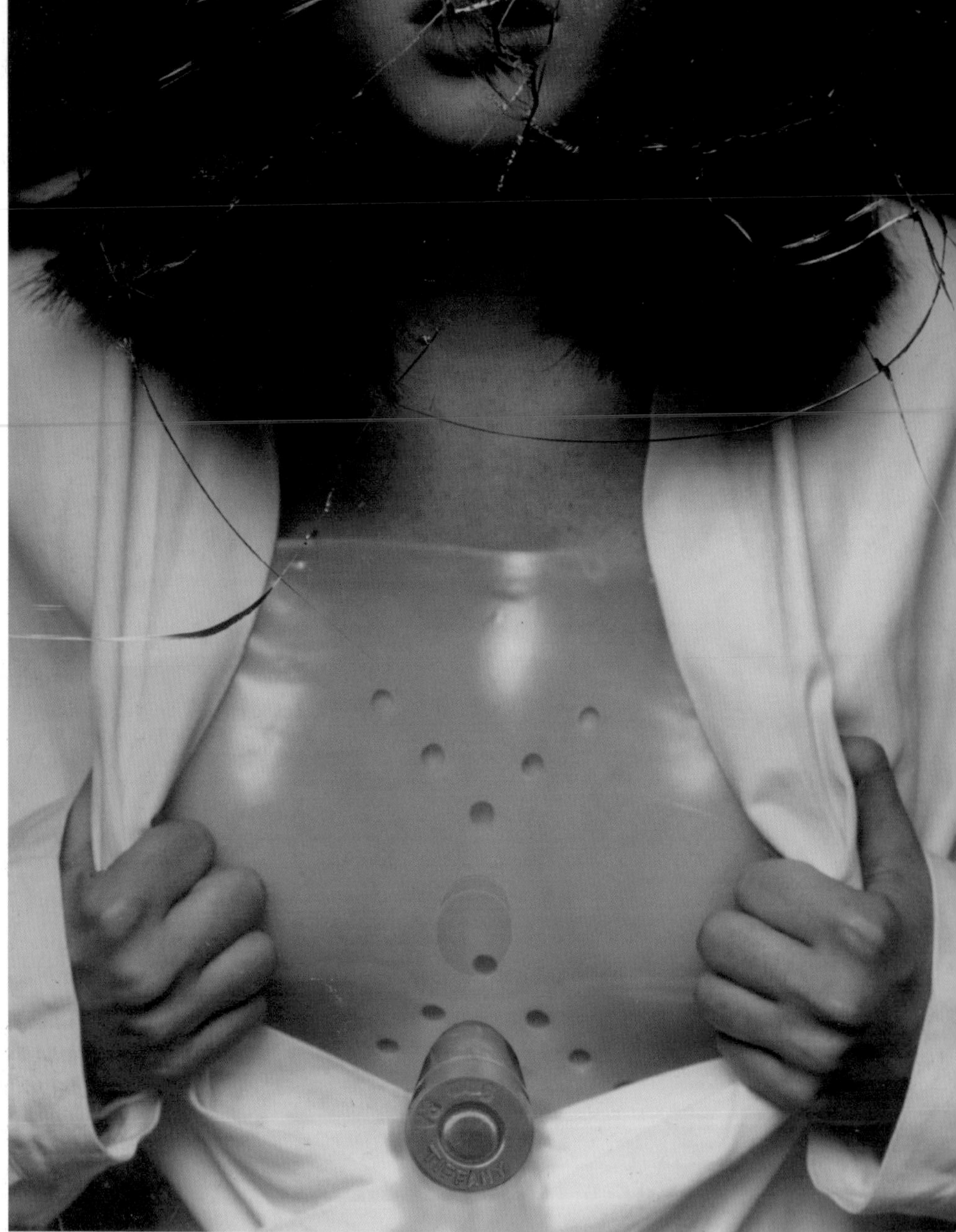

jonathan west

styling: Maria Serra
hair: Taku
make-up: Angela Chung
models: Amy + Emma @ Models 1 + Barbara @ Select

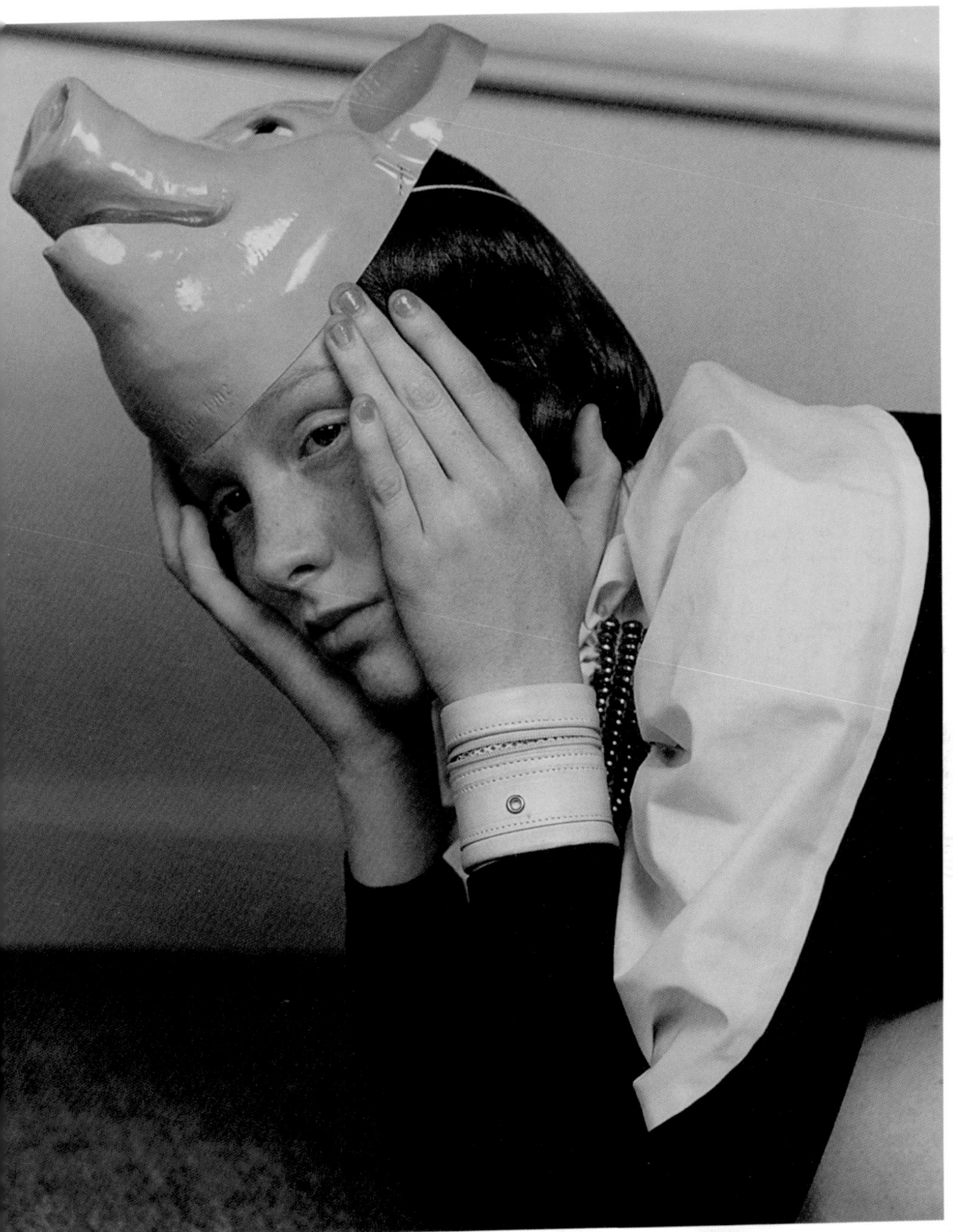

jordis schlösser

April 1999

lisa yuskavage

@ Greengrassi Gallery

marcus tomlinson

hair: Peter Grey
make-up: Hina Dohi

michael danner

styling: Atlanta Rascher
hair: Andrea Panté

michael wilson

@ Nylon Gallery, London

April 1999

MECHANICAL BUT CHARMING
SUSPICIOUS OF NATURE
IMPISH
Schwan Stabilo Swano UNLISTED
KINKY DIRTY
RESIGNED AND MISGUIDED
SUSPICIOUSLY CAREFREE
MONEYED
NEVER LESS THAN INCOHERENT
EXCLUDED
NOT PARANOID ENOUGH
FAIR DINKUM
SHAMBLING
PO-FACED
IMPERVIOUS
ILLUSTRATED
UNPREPOSESSING
FAZED
UNTOUCHABLE
BEAUTIFIC
ATAVISTIC
INVENTED (OF NECESSITY)
FEEBLE
MOST LIKELY TO
CHOKED
DIALLED
OUTRE
CHURLISH
FULLY REPRESENTED
STRAIGHT OUTTA
SCALY
VIRTUAL
GUSHING WITH SENTIMENT
TOP-FLIGHT
FOPPISH
ACID, SALTY
HELL-BENT

olivier bouché

styling: Delphine Pavy
hair: Ed Mollands
make-up: Alex
models: Saimic @ Next · Amy Nemee + Marie @ City

oscar stevenson

rock

pop

jazz

simon leigh

April 1999

stephan vanfleteren

stephen gill

461

USTAL

craft works.

issue 5, July 1999, cover photo by John-Paul Pietrus

alexandra kinga fekete

@ Caroline McCabe

7

brock elbank

styling: Jo Phillips
hair: Craig Mason
make-up: Linda Burns

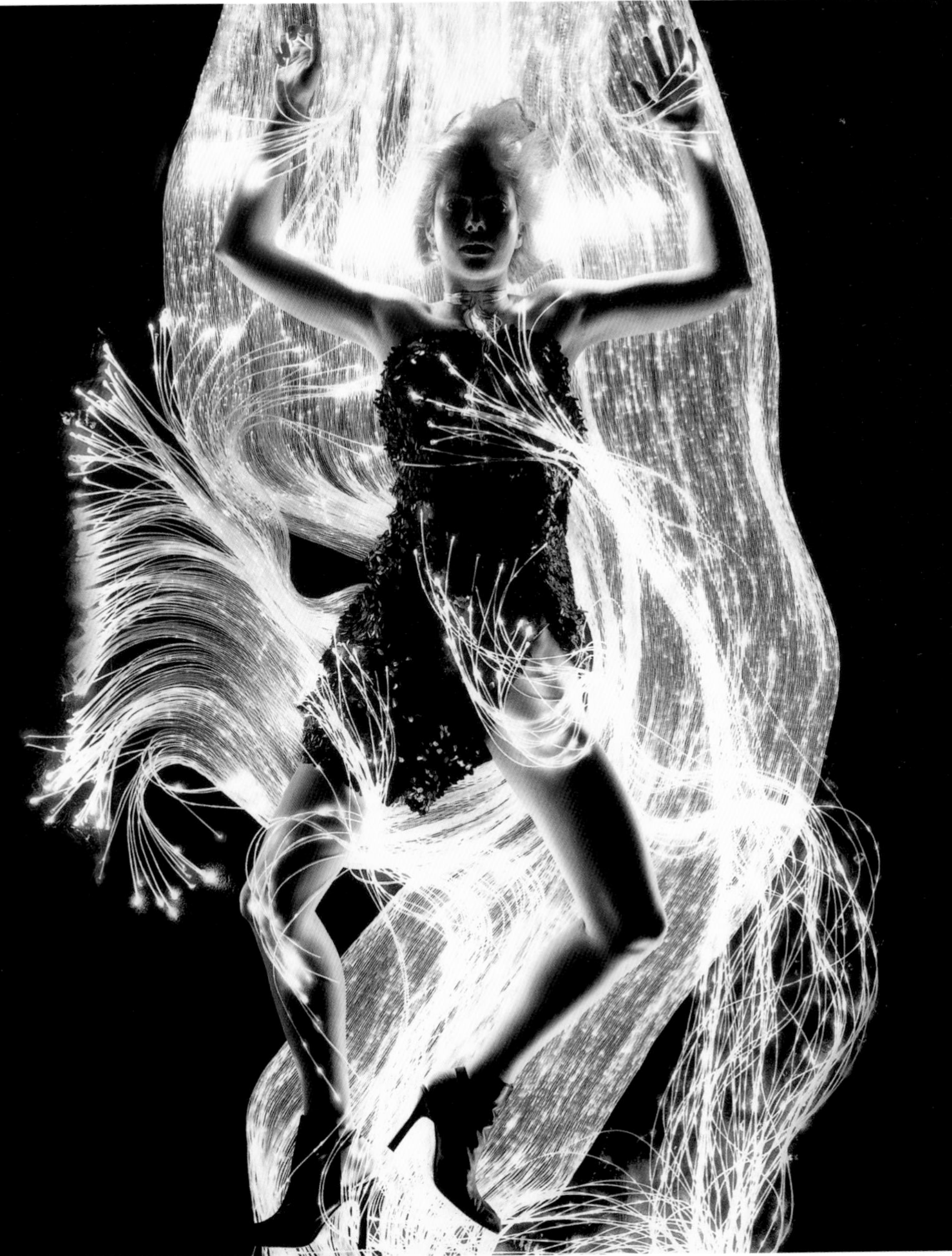

laurent croisier

styling: Luciano Neves
hair: Alexis
make-up: Maya
model: Mai-Anh Le @ Ford

July 1999

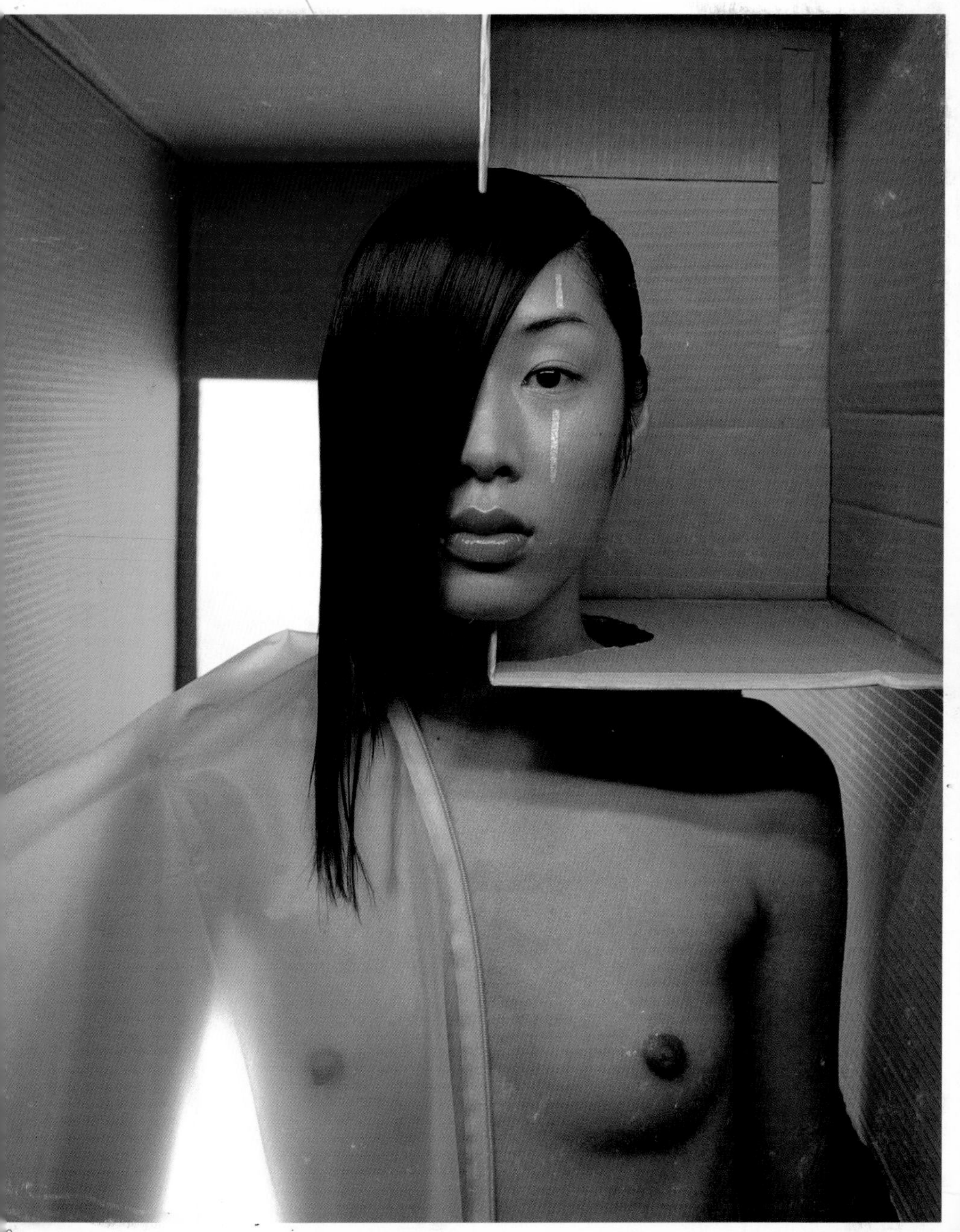

john-paul pietrus

styling: Sophia Neophitou
hair: Jennie Roberts
make-up: Liz Martins
model: Ira @ Models 1

1

thank you!

SHOWING LIVE
24 7
FUNKIEST

jonathan west

styling: Maria Serra
hair: Taku
make-up: Angela Chung
model: Kirsten Pieters @ Take 2

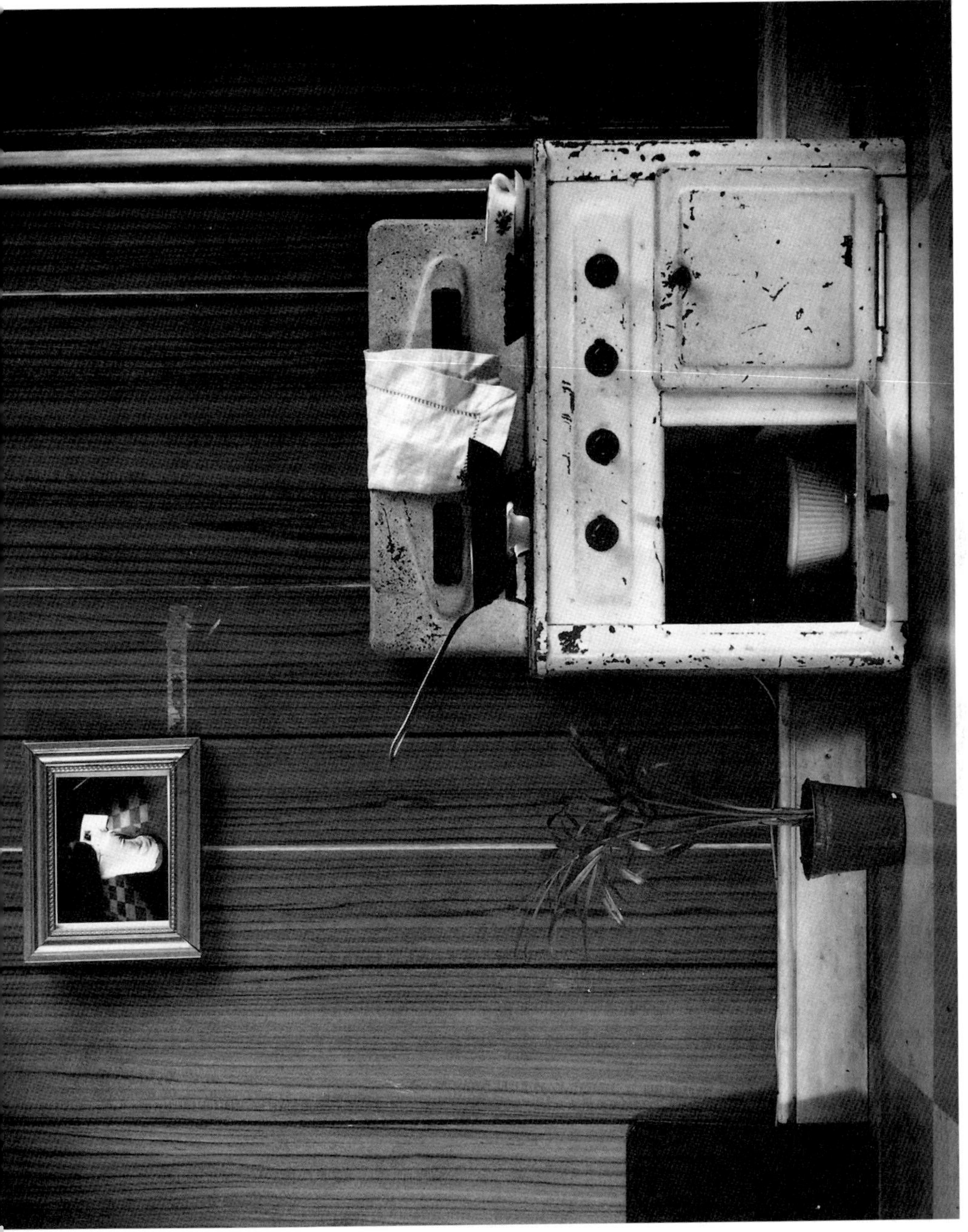

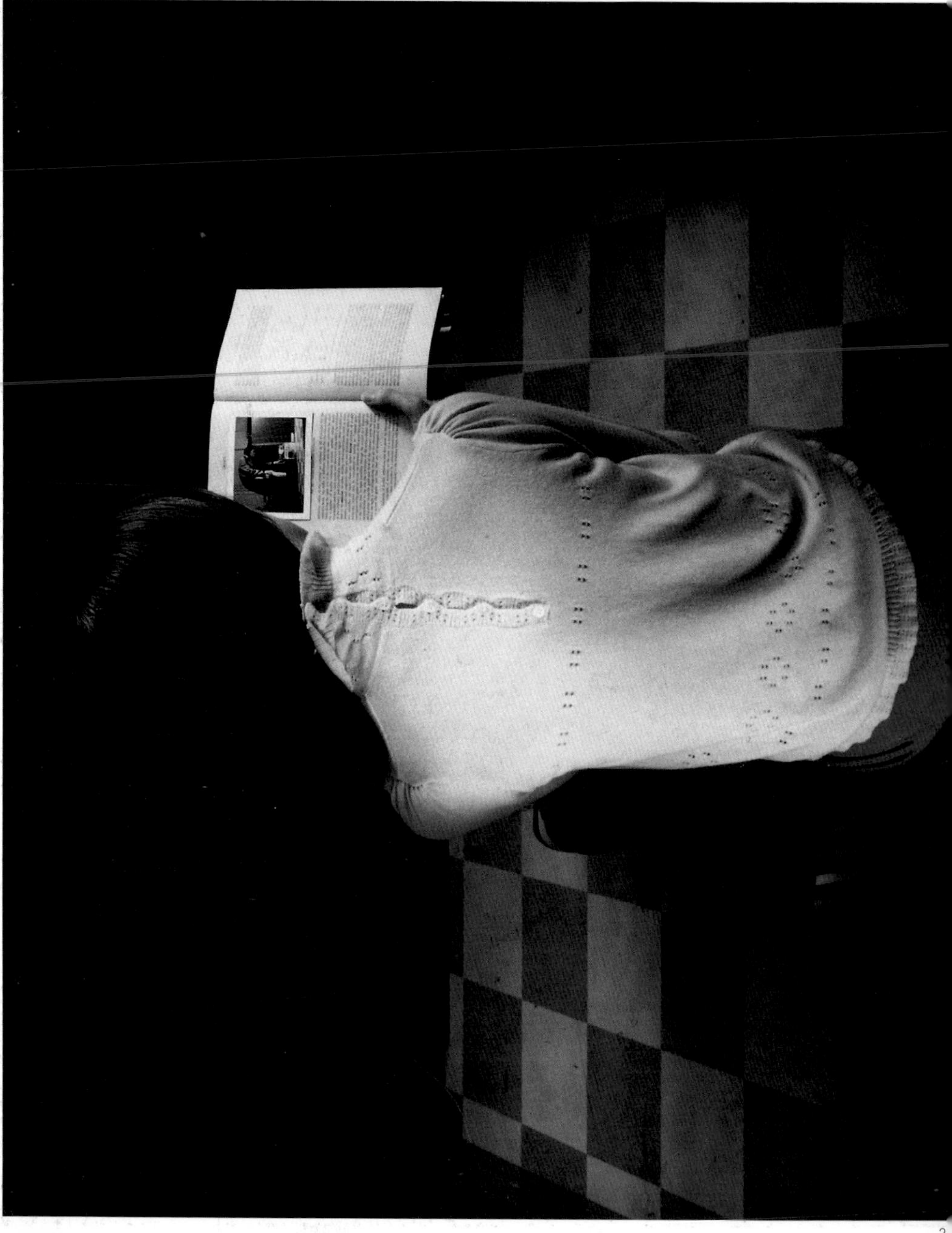

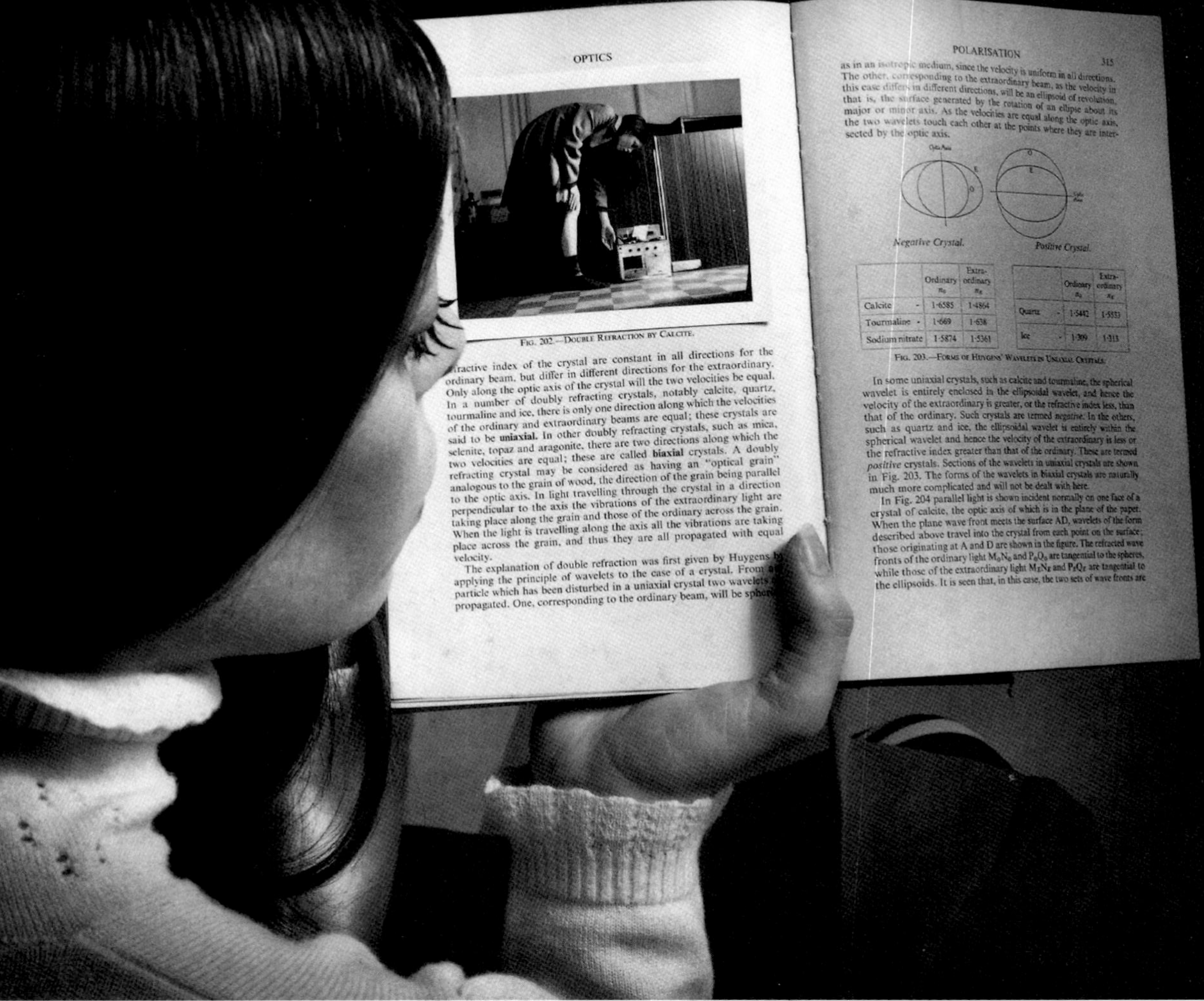
OPTICS
FIG. 202.—DOUBLE REFRACTION BY CALCITE.
fractive index of the crystal are constant in all directions for the ordinary beam, but differ in different directions for the extraordinary. Only along the optic axis of the crystal will the two velocities be equal. In a number of doubly refracting crystals, notably calcite, quartz, tourmaline and ice, there is only one direction along which the velocities of the ordinary and extraordinary beams are equal; these crystals are said to be uniaxial. In other doubly refracting crystals, such as mica, selenite, topaz and aragonite, there are two directions along which the two velocities are equal; these are called biaxial crystals. A doubly refracting crystal may be considered as having an "optical grain" analogous to the grain of wood, the direction of the grain being parallel to the optic axis. In light travelling through the crystal in a direction perpendicular to the axis the vibrations of the extraordinary light are taking place along the grain and those of the ordinary across the grain. When the light is travelling along the axis all the vibrations are taking place across the grain, and thus they are all propagated with equal velocity.
The explanation of double refraction was first given by Huygens by applying the principle of wavelets to the case of a crystal. From a particle which has been disturbed in a uniaxial crystal two wavelets propagated. One, corresponding to the ordinary beam, will be spher
POLARISATION
315
as in an isotropic medium, since the velocity is uniform in all directions. The other, corresponding to the extraordinary beam, as the velocity in this case differs in different directions, will be an ellipsoid of revolution, that is, the surface generated by the rotation of an ellipse about its major or minor axis. As the velocities are equal along the optic axis, the two wavelets touch each other at the points where they are intersected by the optic axis.
Negative Crystal.
Positive Crystal.
Ordinary n_0 | Extra-ordinary n_E
Calcite - 1·6585 1·4864
Tourmaline - 1·669 1·638
Sodium nitrate 1·5874 1·5361
Quartz - 1·5442 1·5533
Ice - 1·309 1·313
FIG. 203.—FORMS OF HUYGENS' WAVELETS IN UNIAXIAL CRYSTALS.
In some uniaxial crystals, such as calcite and tourmaline, the spherical wavelet is entirely enclosed in the ellipsoidal wavelet, and hence the velocity of the extraordinary is greater, or the refractive index less, than that of the ordinary. Such crystals are termed negative. In the others, such as quartz and ice, the ellipsoidal wavelet is entirely within the spherical wavelet and hence the velocity of the extraordinary is less or the refractive index greater than that of the ordinary. These are termed positive crystals. Sections of the wavelets in uniaxial crystals are shown in Fig. 203. The forms of the wavelets in biaxial crystals are naturally much more complicated and will not be dealt with here.
In Fig. 204 parallel light is shown incident normally on one face of a crystal of calcite, the optic axis of which is in the plane of the paper. When the plane wave front meets the surface AD, wavelets of the form described above travel into the crystal from each point on the surface; those originating at A and D are shown in the figure. The refracted wave fronts of the ordinary light M_0N_0 and P_0Q_0 are tangential to the spheres, while those of the extraordinary light M_EN_E and P_EQ_E are tangential to the ellipsoids. It is seen that, in this case, the two sets of wave fronts are

FIG. 202.—DOUBLE REFRACTION BY CALCITE.

refractive index of the crystal are constant in all directions for the ordinary beam, but differ in different directions for the extraordinary. Only along the optic axis of the crystal will the two velocities be equal. In a number of doubly refracting crystals, notably calcite, quartz, tourmaline and ice, there is only one direction along which the velocities of the ordinary and extraordinary beams are equal; these crystals are said to be **uniaxial.** In other doubly refracting crystals, such as mica, selenite, topaz and aragonite, there are two directions along which the two velocities are equal; these are called **biaxial** crystals. A doubly refracting crystal may be considered as having an "optical grain" analogous to the grain of wood, the direction of the grain being parallel to the optic axis. In light travelling through the crystal in a direction perpendicular to the axis the vibrations of the extraordinary light are taking place along the grain and those of the ordinary across the grain.

masoud

styling: Charty Durrant
hair: Kevin Ford
make-up: Charlotte Day
model: Zoya @ Models 1

vincent gallo

@ Lotta Hammer Gallery, London

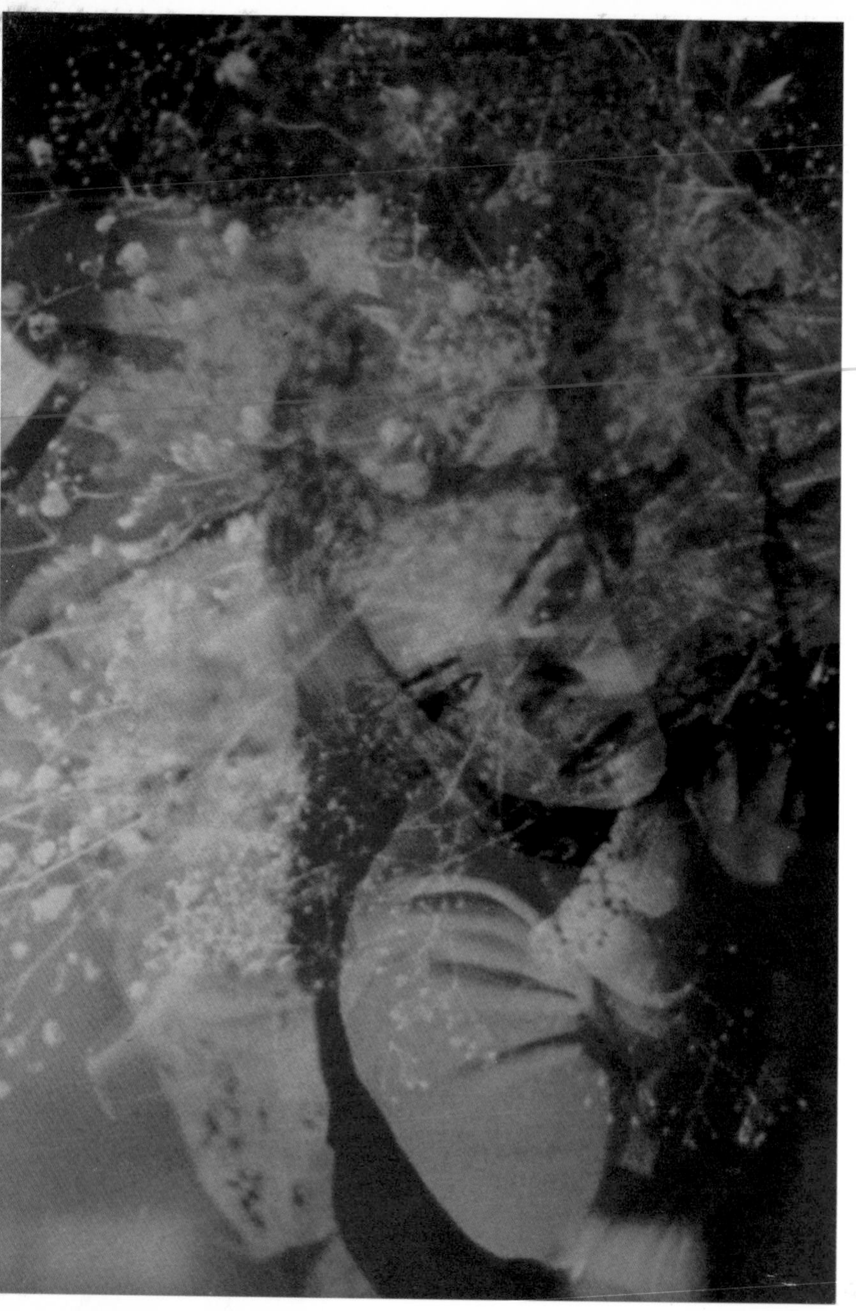

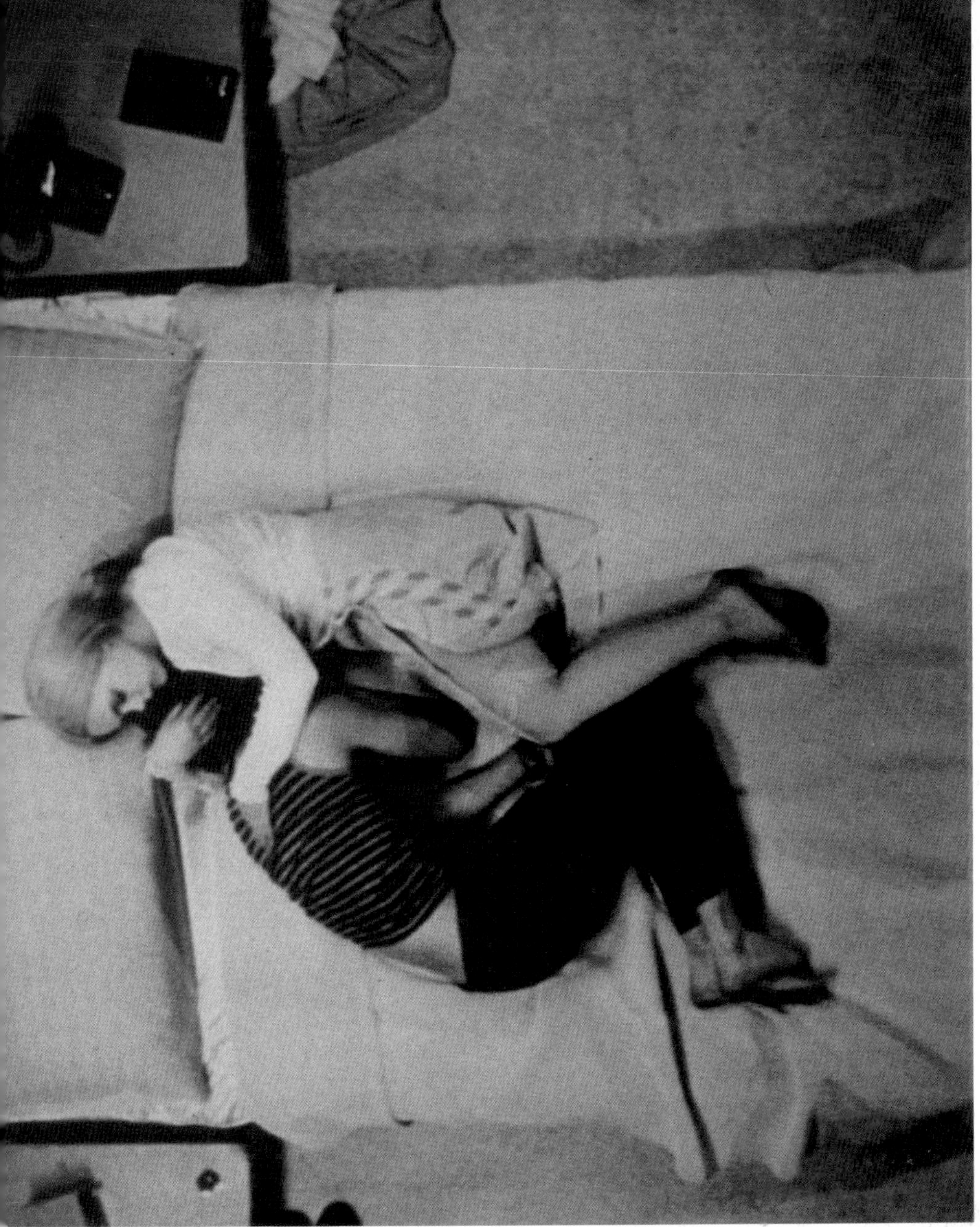

nute nicholson

styling: Claudia Carretti
hair: Pierluigi Tavelli
make-up: Cristine Du-Puys
model: Kirsten P. @ Take 2

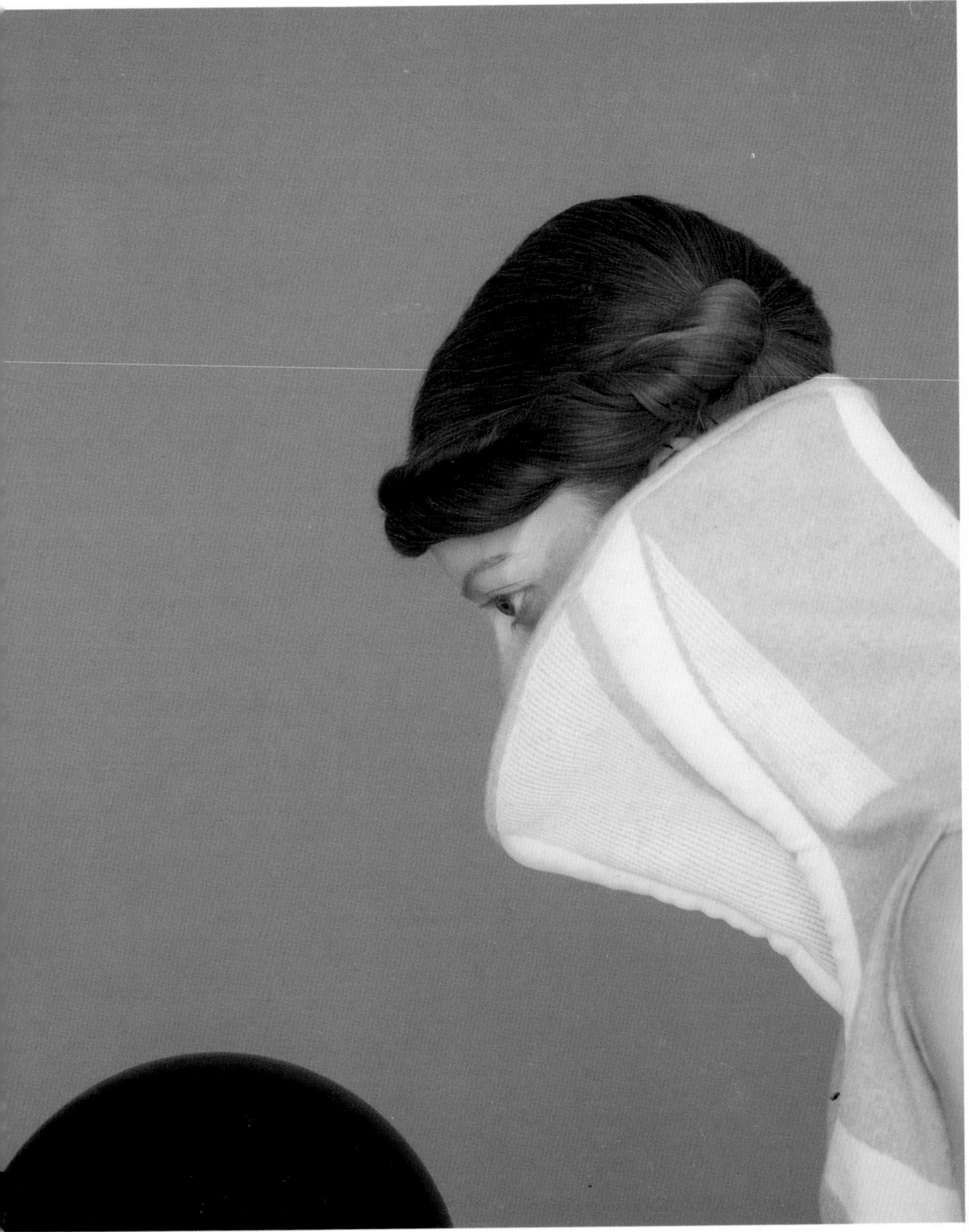

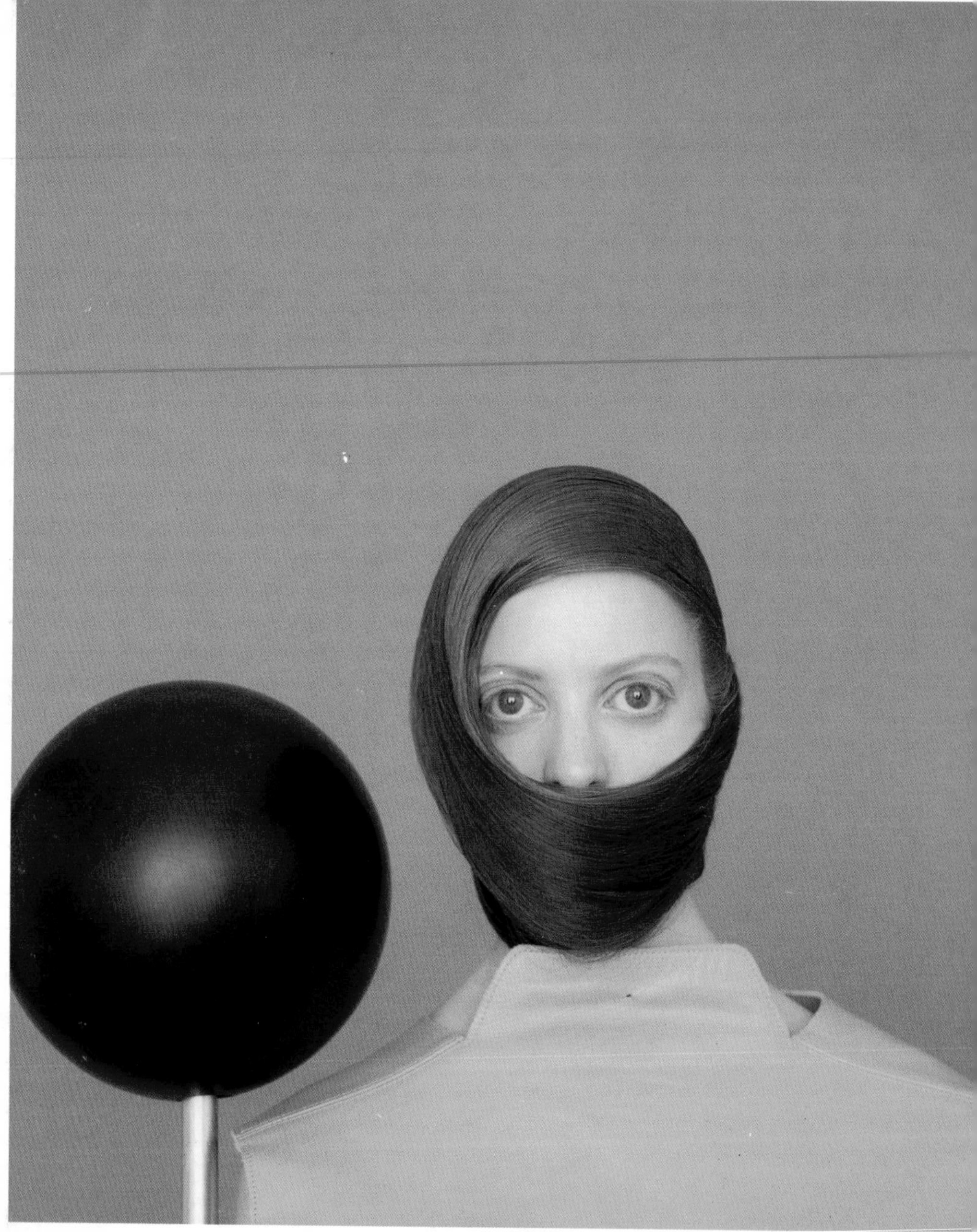

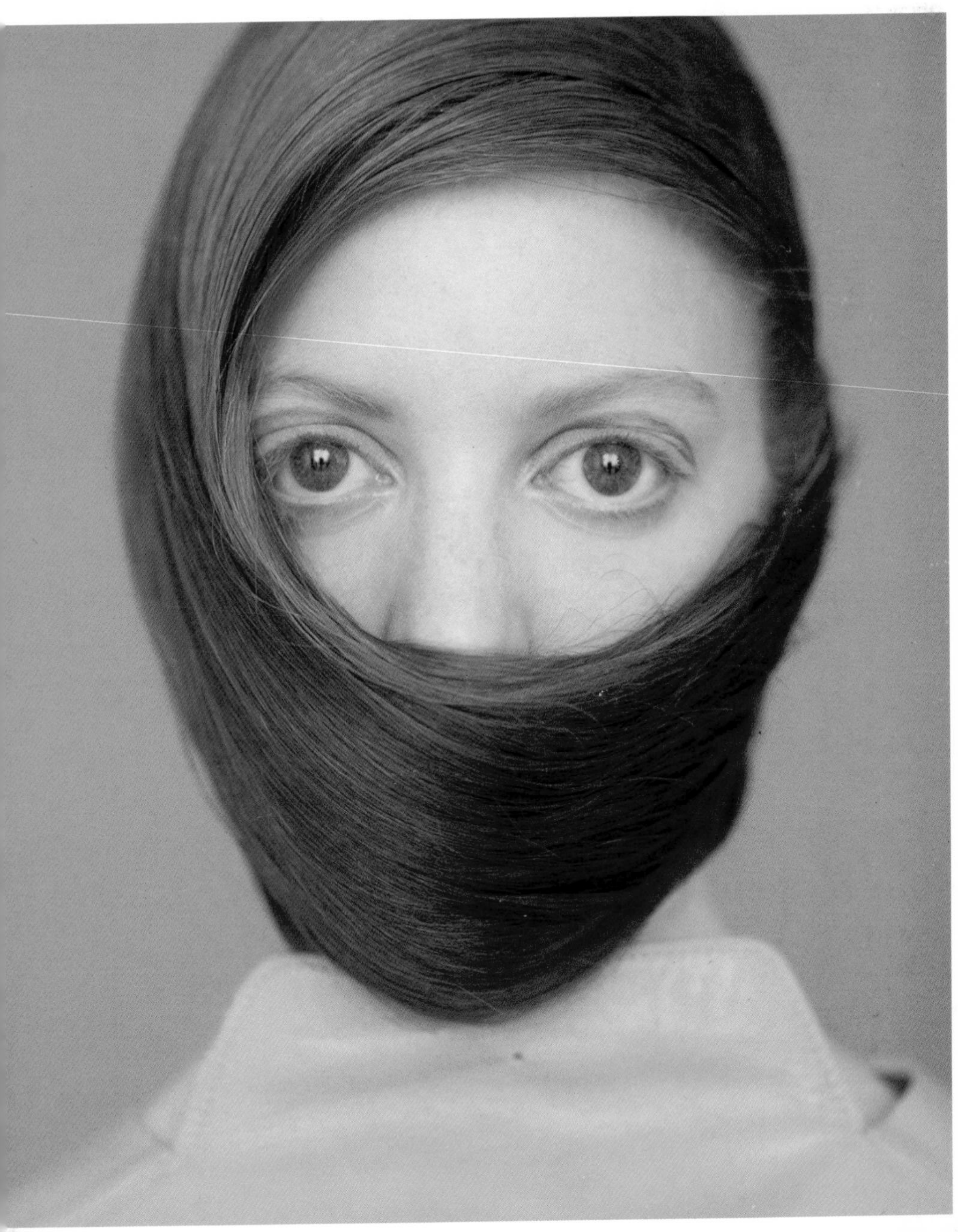

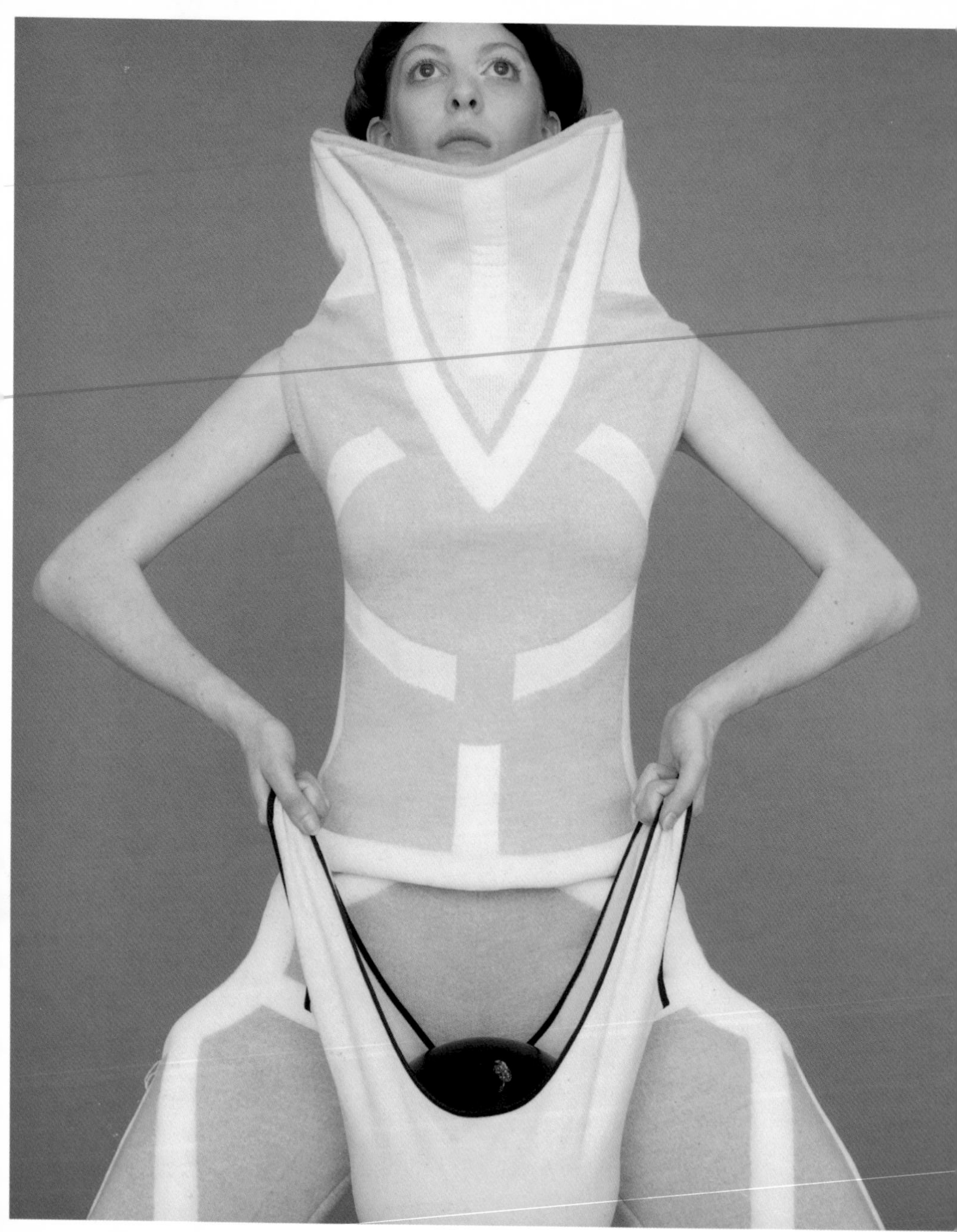

tim bret-day

styling: Faye Sawyer

masoud

beauty: Topolino
styling: Giannie Couji
hair: Fouad
models: Helen + Valeria @ Premiere

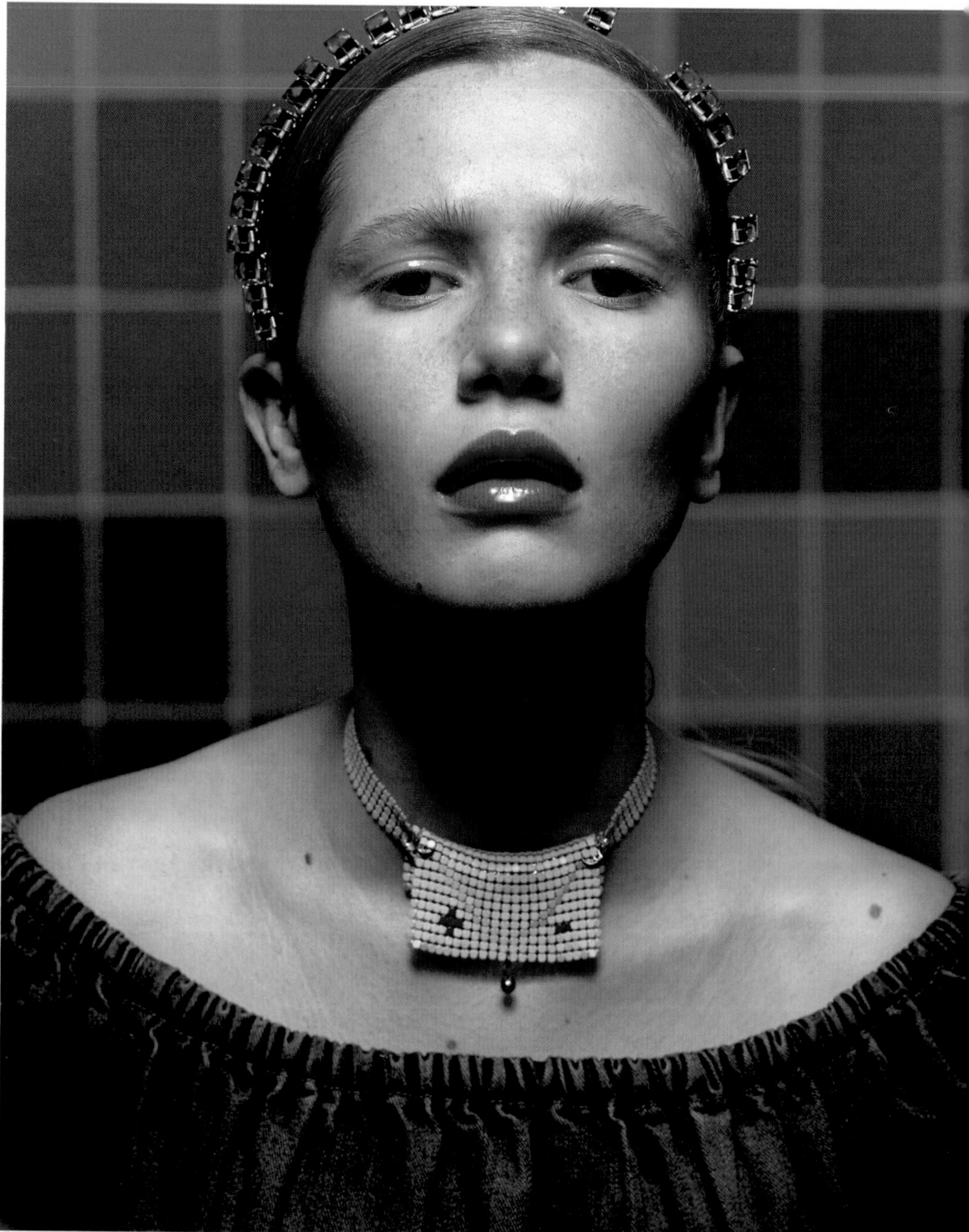

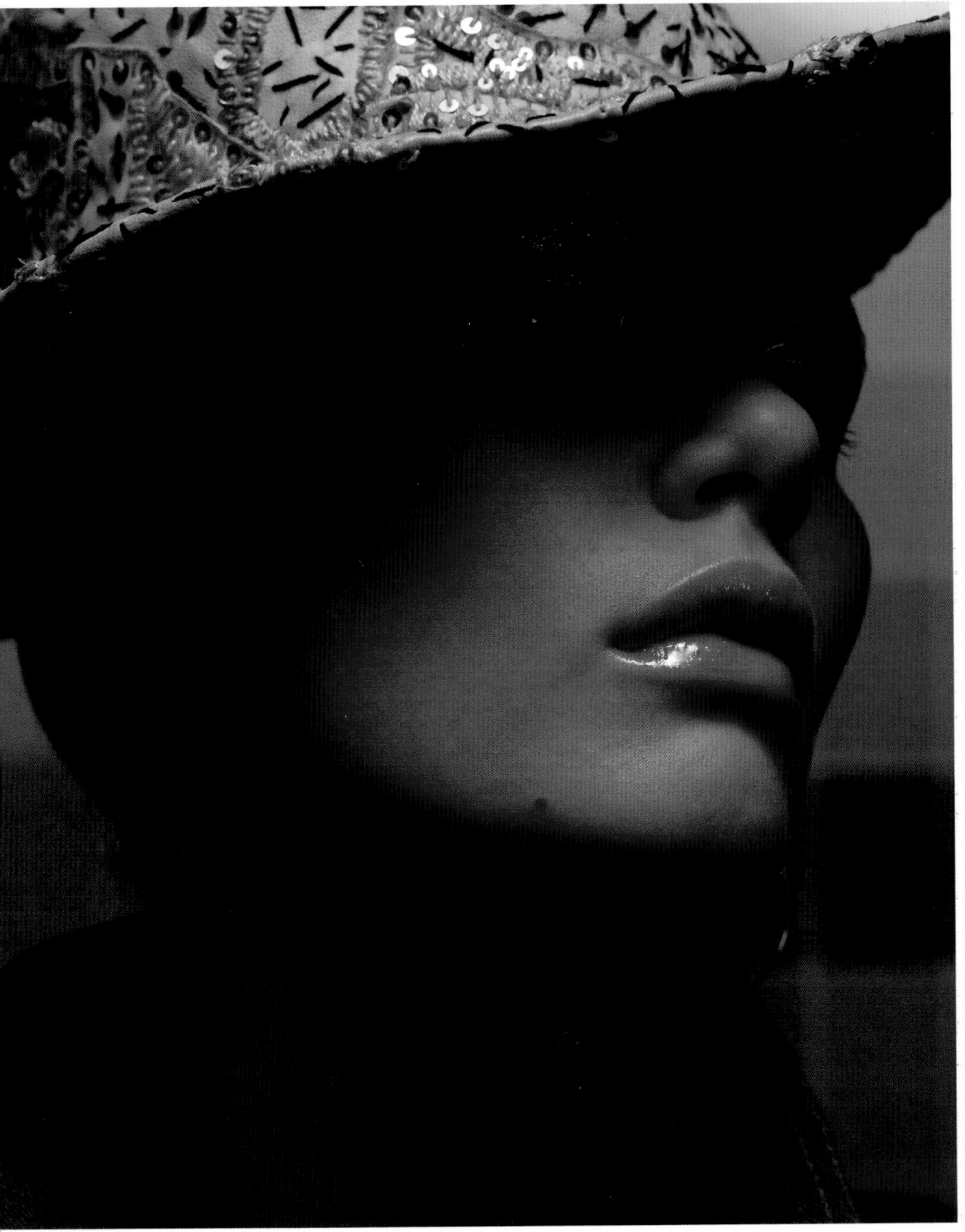

we're in a wide open space.

issue 6, September 1999, cover photo by Thierry van Biesen

charles avery

@ Percy Miller Gallery, London

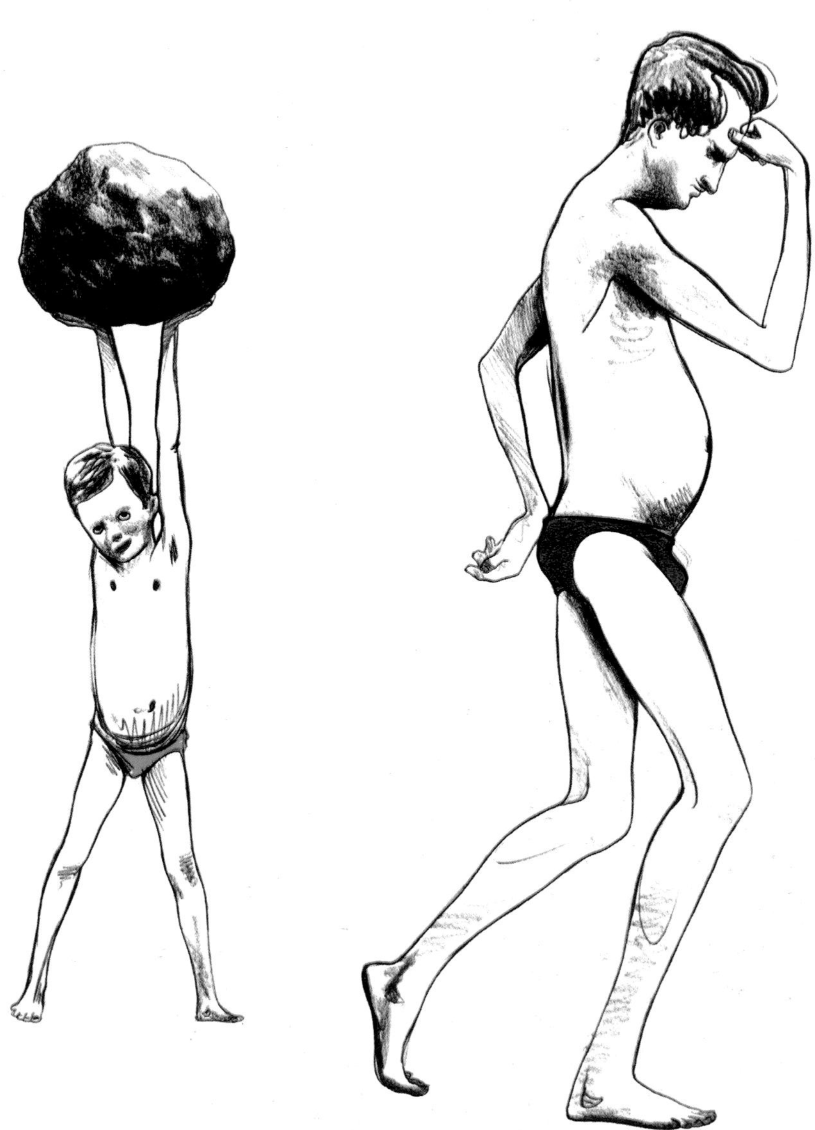

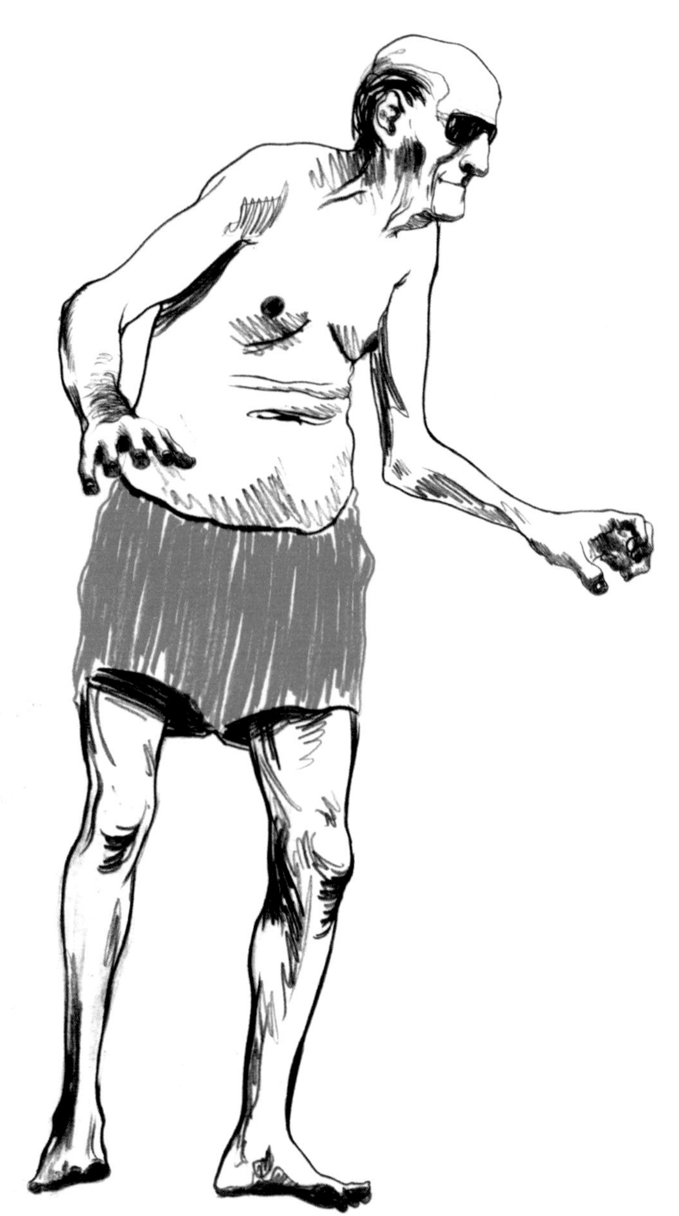

david oldham

styling: snatch
hair: Callum
make-up: Adam de Cruz

gottfried helnwein

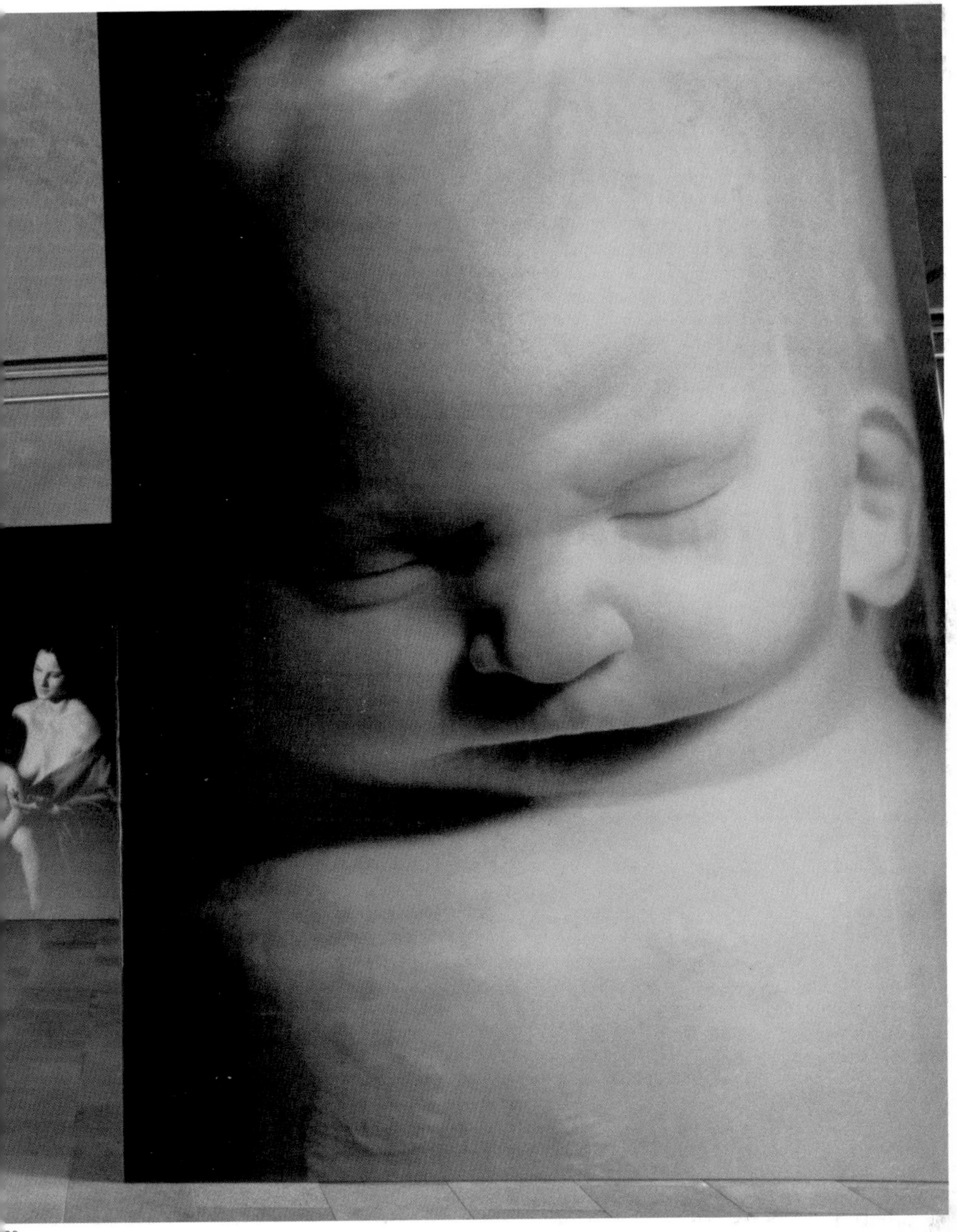

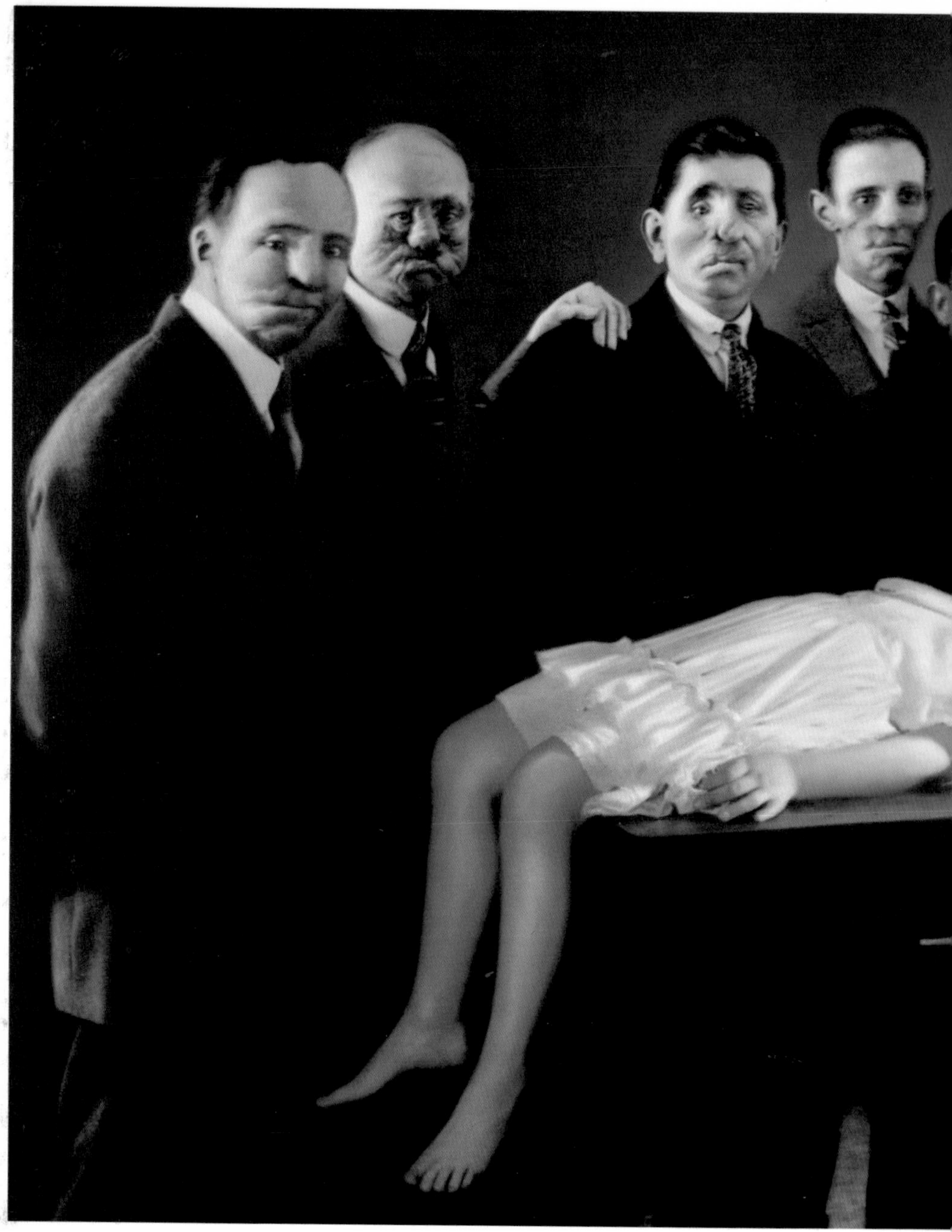

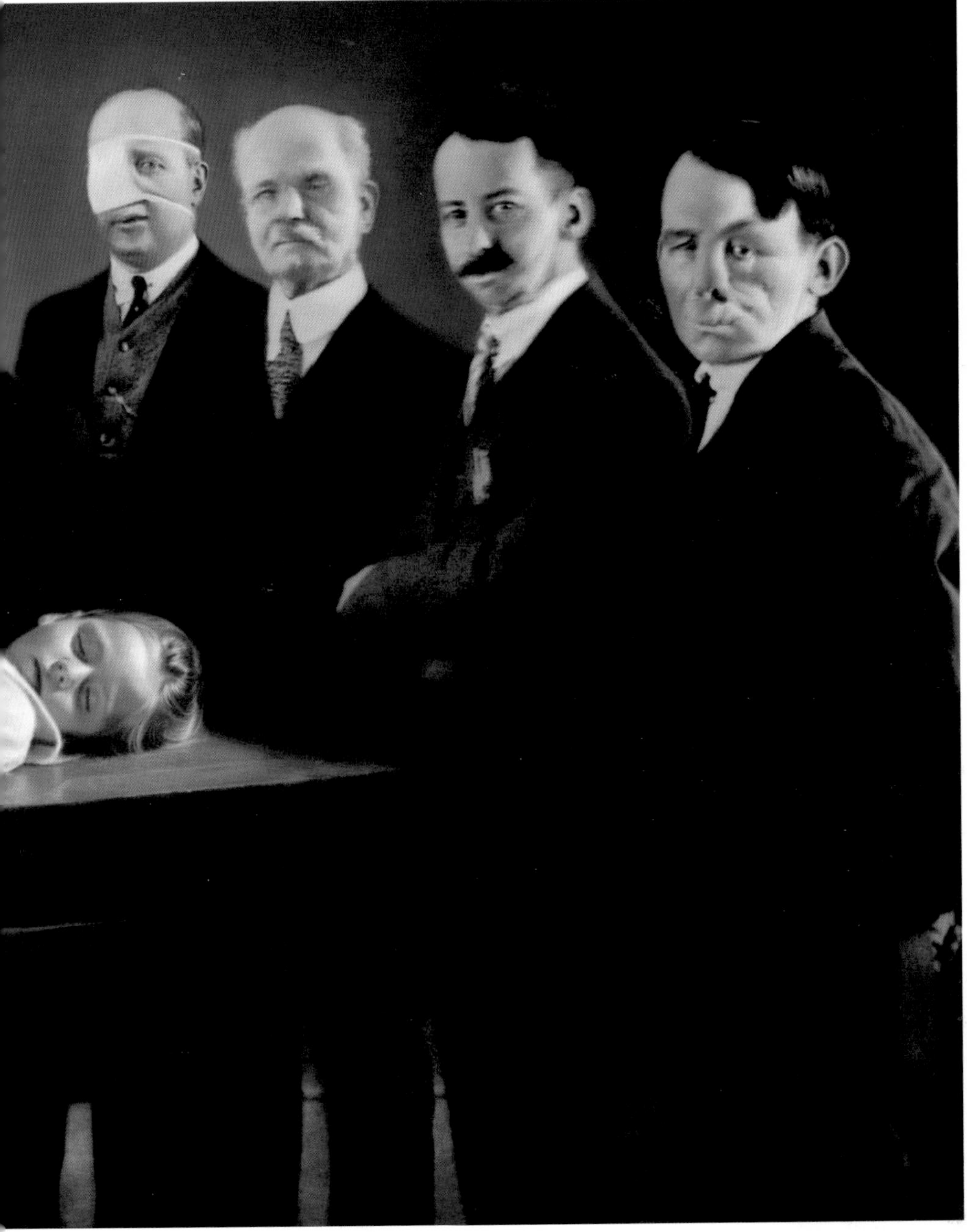

heiko fischer

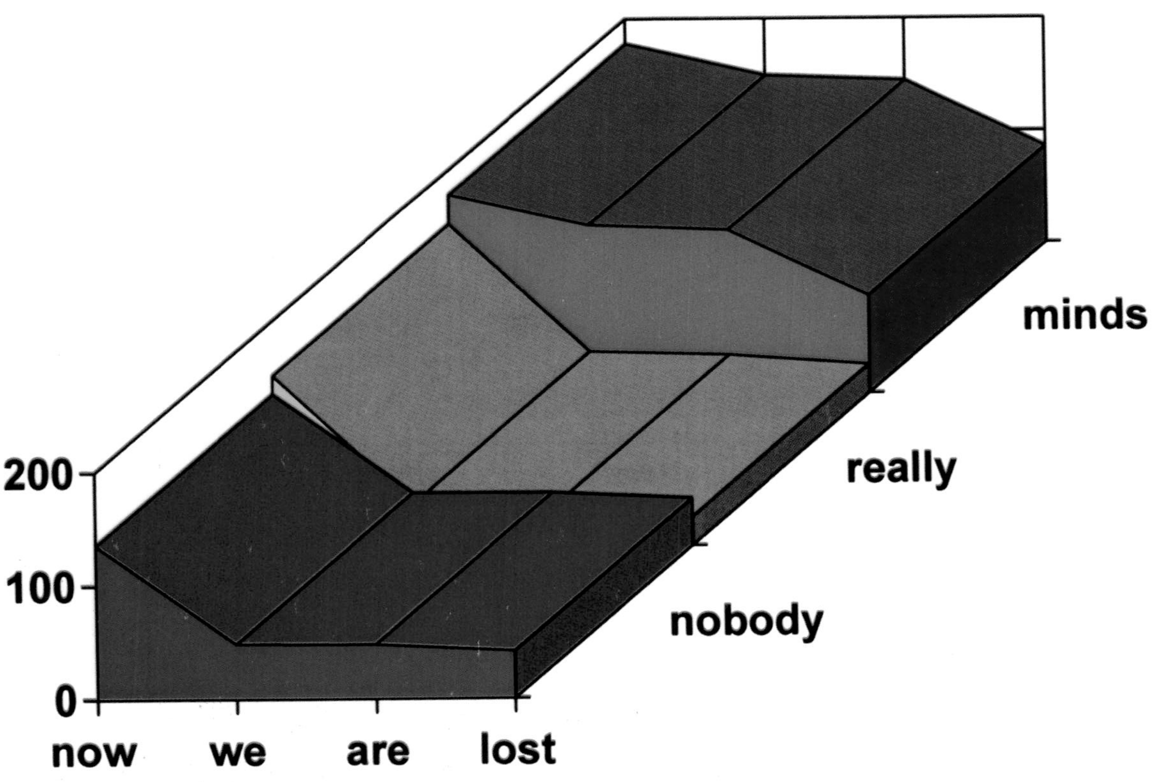
200
100
0
now
we
are
lost
nobody
really
minds

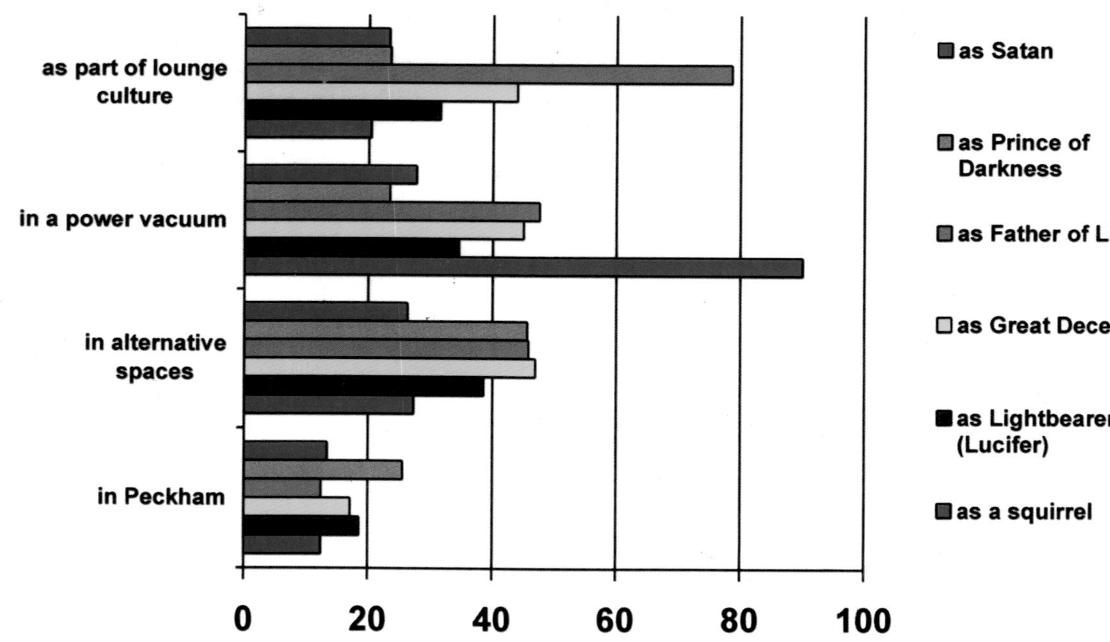
sightings of the Devil in 1999
as part of lounge culture
in a power vacuum
in alternative spaces
in Peckham
0
20
40
60
80
100
as Satan
as Prince of Darkness
as Father of Lies
as Great Deceiver
as Lightbearer (Lucifer)
as a squirrel

a classic state of being

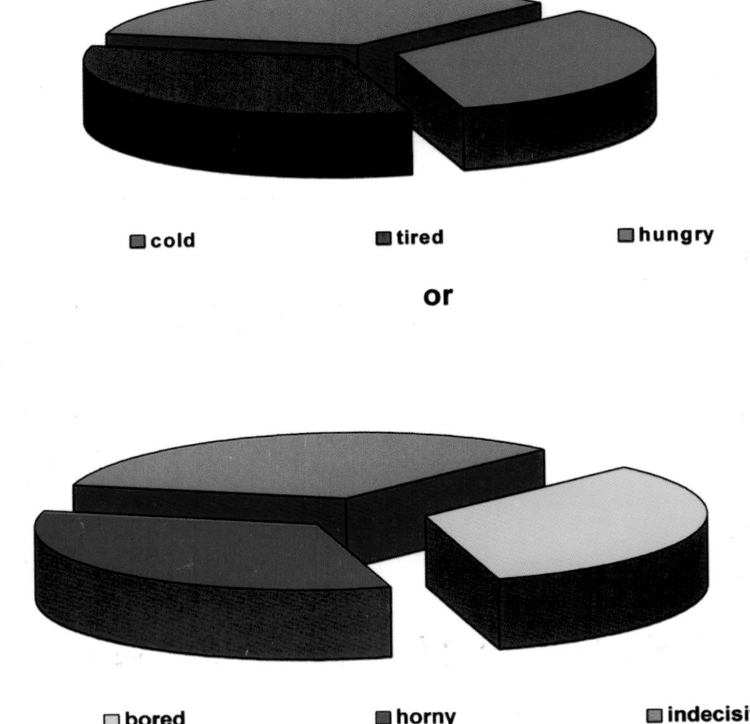

things you

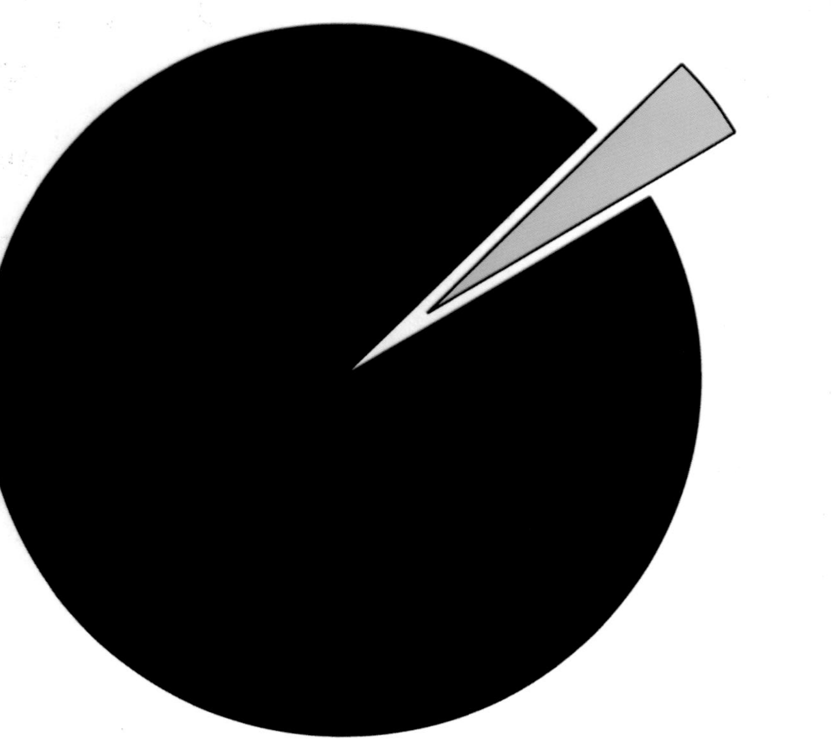

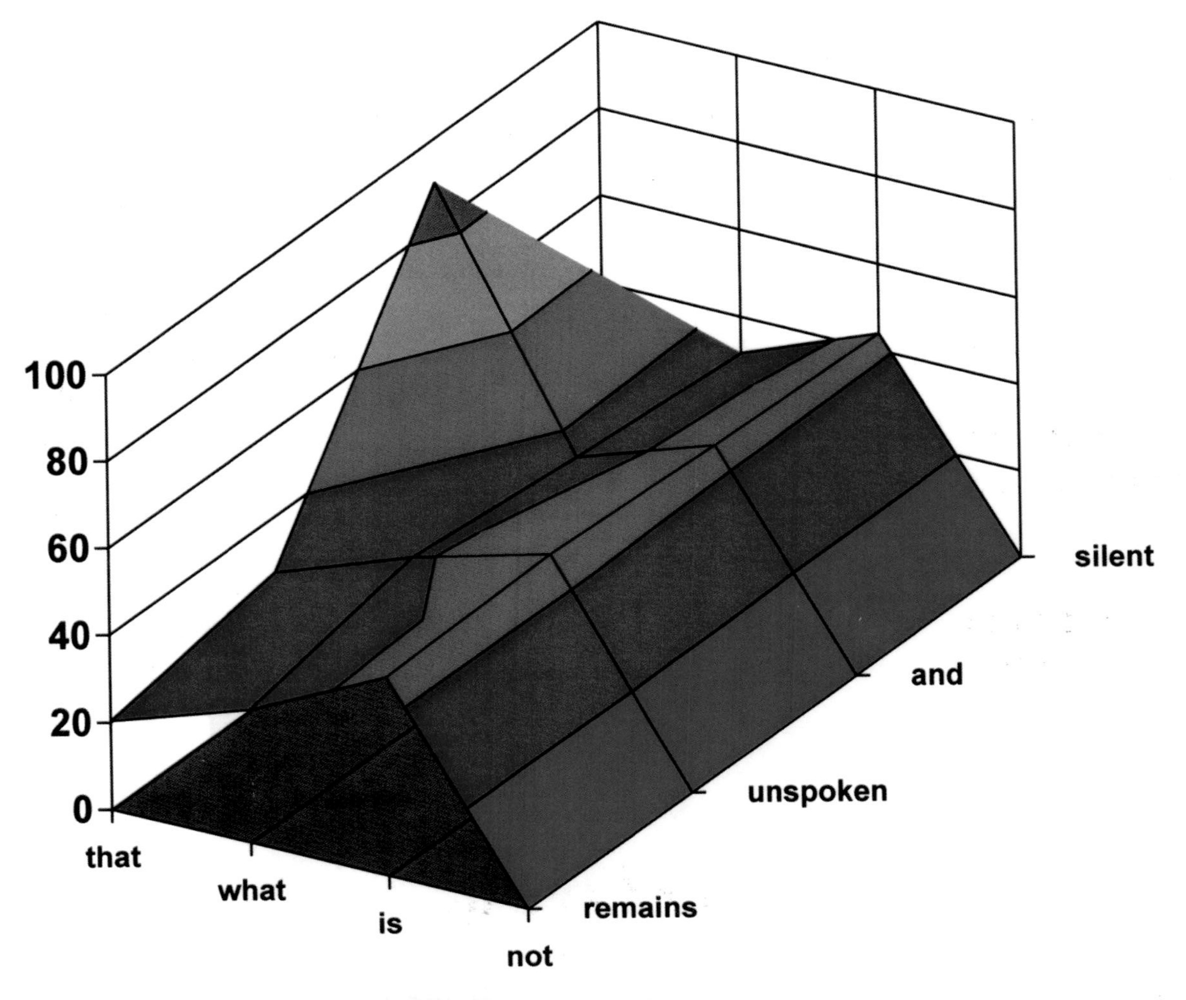
100
80
60
40
20
0
that
what
is
not
remains
unspoken
and
silent

a look at unintended collective consequences of human decisions

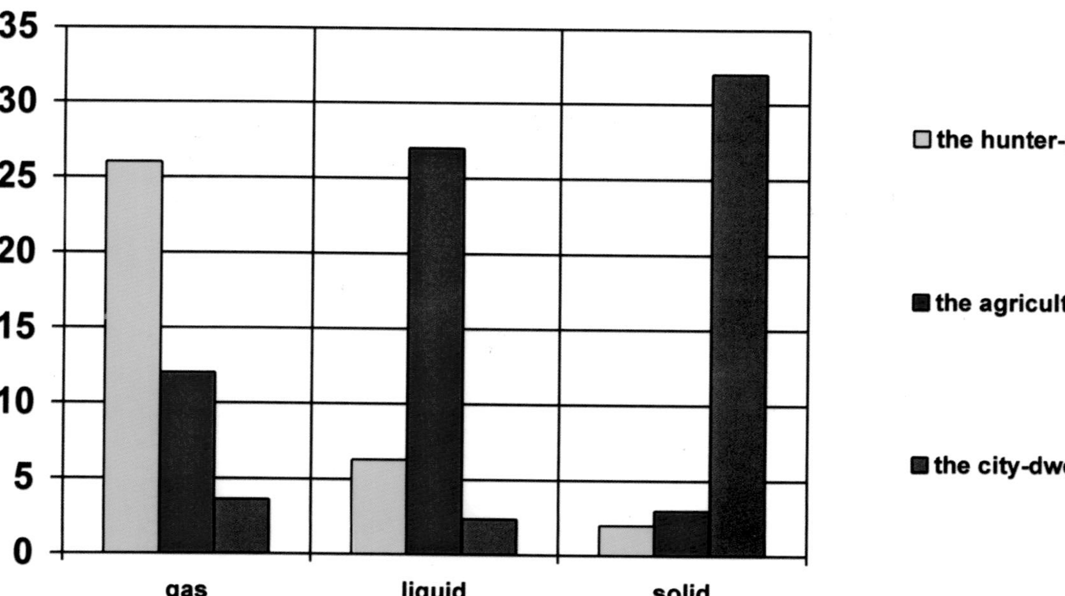

i am
a person
and i
am afraid

a pirate utopia?

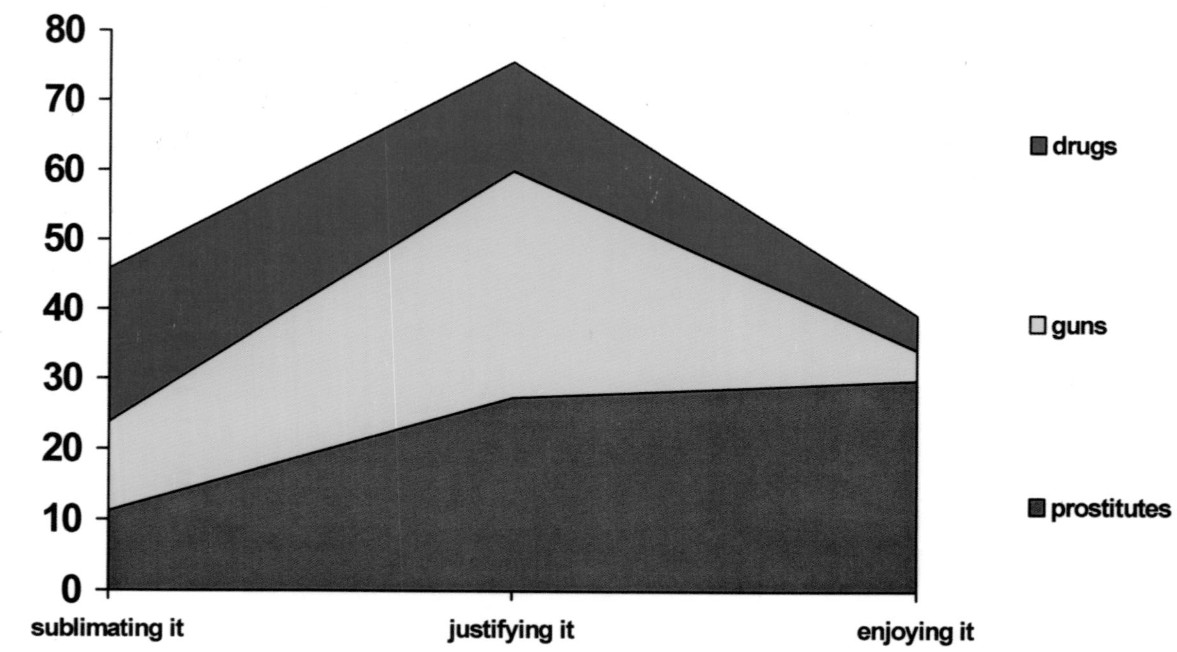

the heartlessness of a brainless world

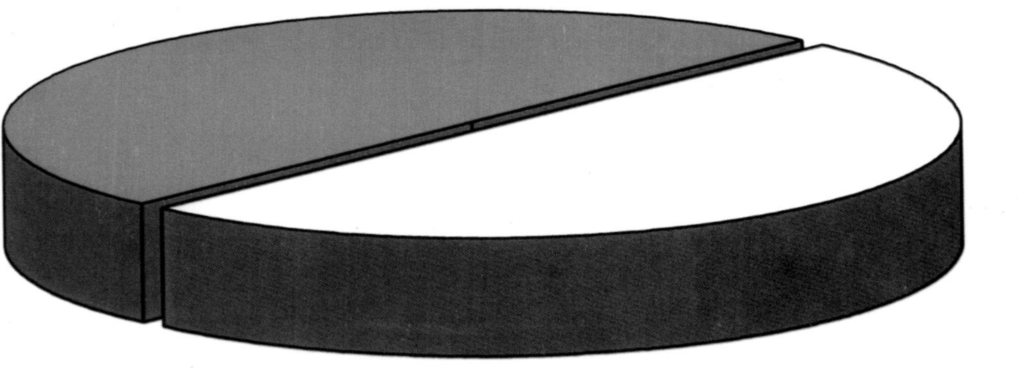

☐ ambient fear ▩ ambient aggression

justine

styling: Faye Sawyer
hair: Fernando Torrent
make-up: Liz Daxauer
set design: Daryl McGregor
models: Sian @ Storm + Chantalle @ Models 1

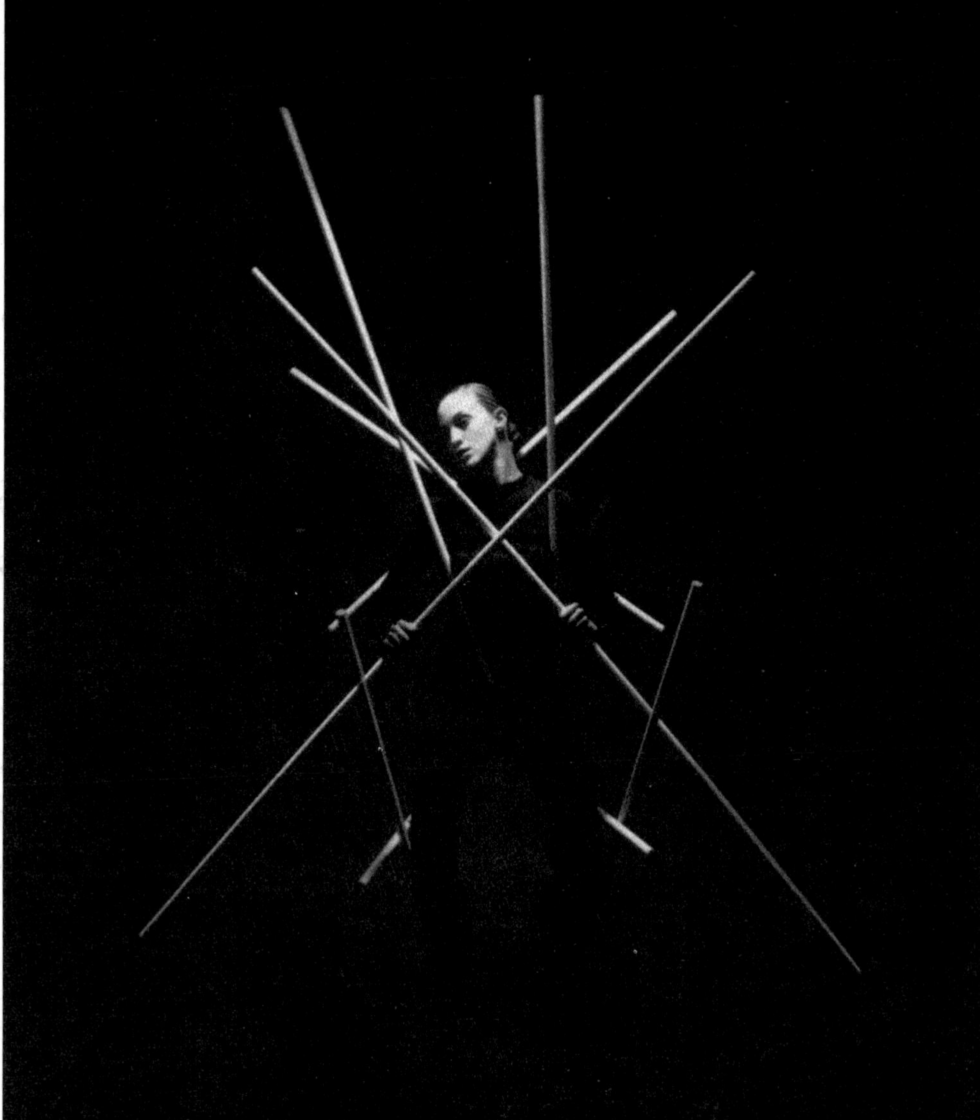

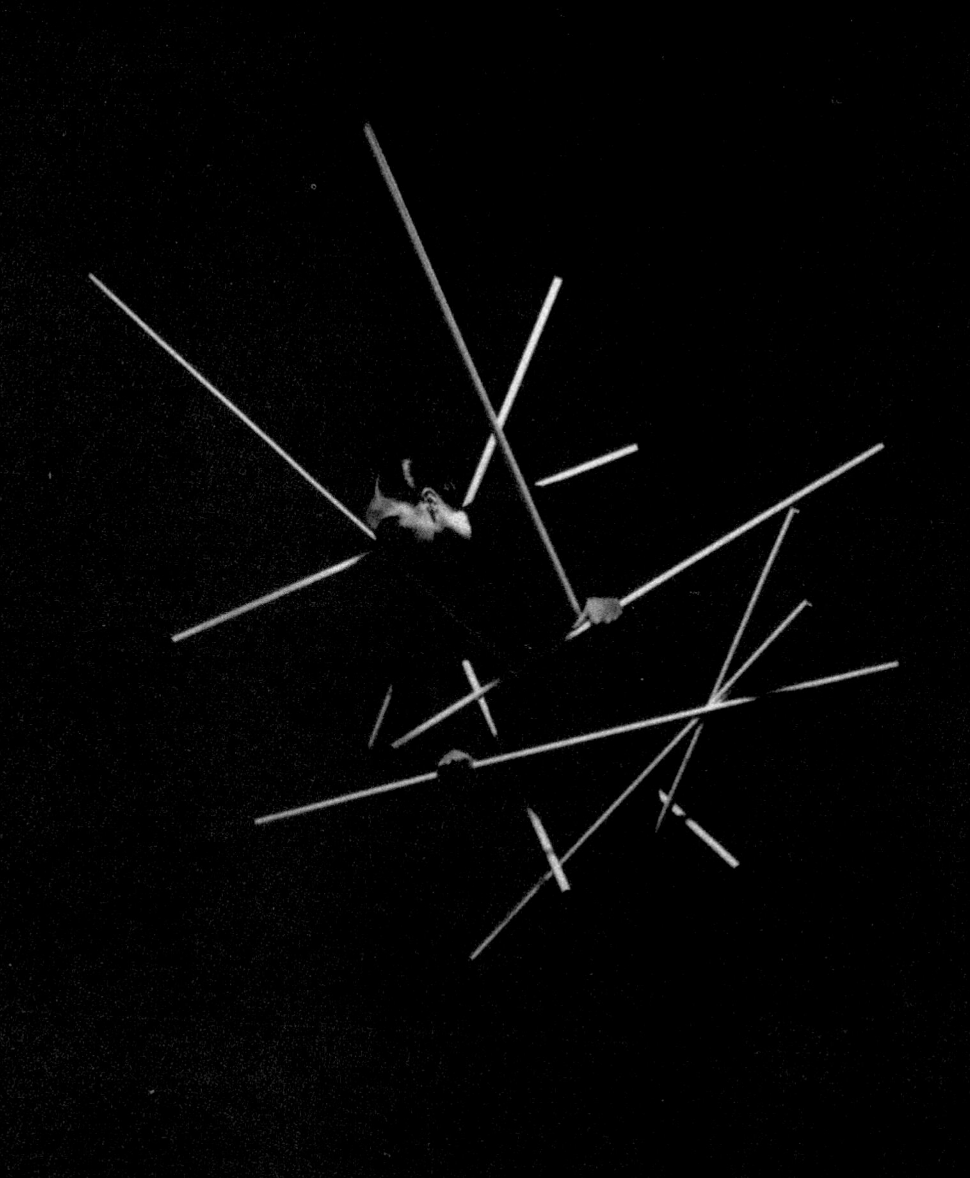

9

1

kai wiechmann

styling: Atlanta Rascher
hair: Andrea Pante
make-up: Dina
models: Lucy + Karri + Khalid

moschinomoschino
mosc
moschino

moschino
moschino

masoud

styling: Frankie Goldstone
hair: Kevin Ford
make-up: Charlotte Day
models: Charlotte B + Laura K @ Models 1 · Victoria Palmer @ Premier
Doug Haywood @ Bookings Men

rikke
ruhwald

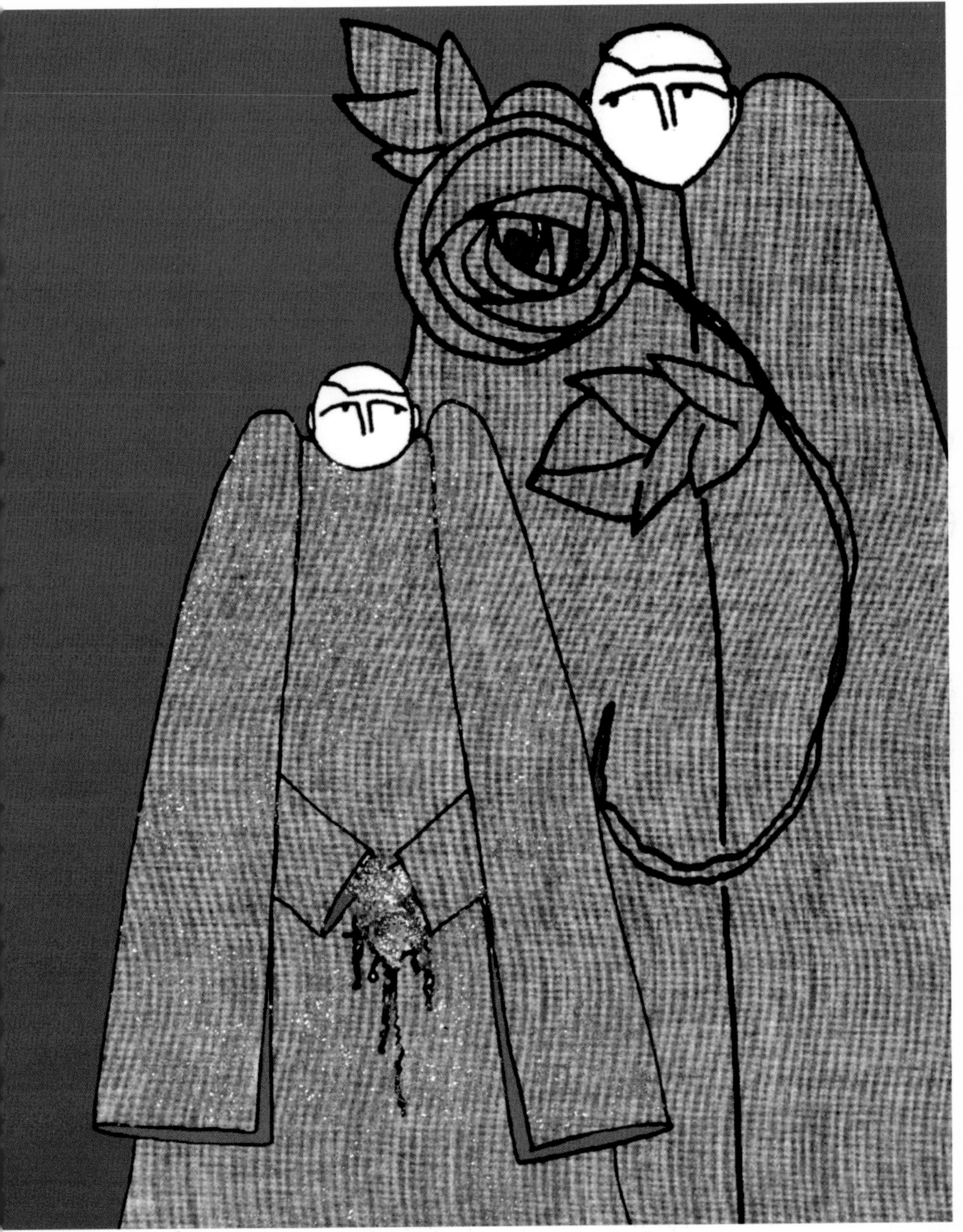

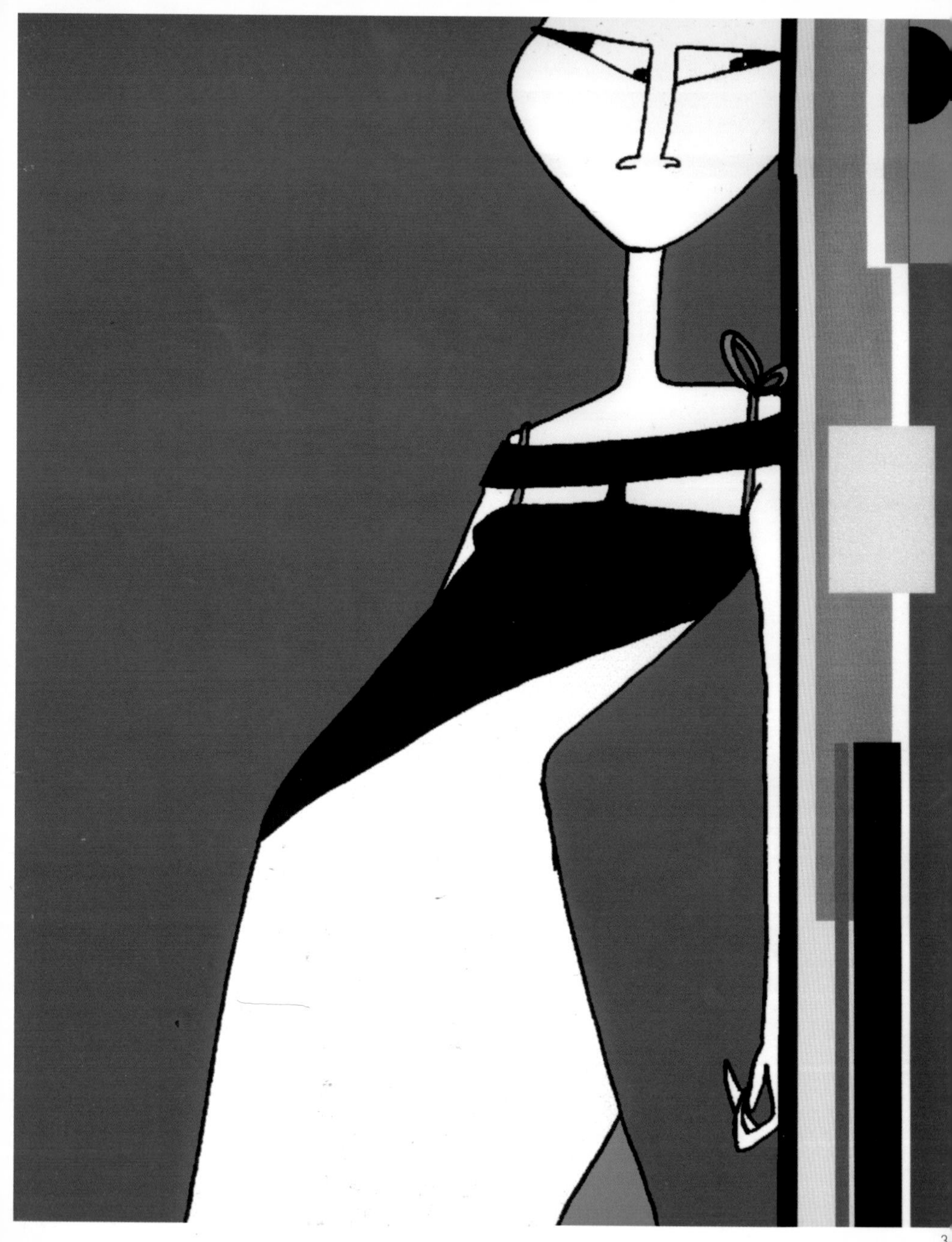

thierry van biesen

styling: Marianne Ghantous
hair: Christophe Martin
make-up: Philippe Miletto
models: Faye · Vanessa + Henry @ Take 2

1

vehicle

September 1999

Goodge St
BEDFORD SQ
DEAN

Adhafera
NCG3344
CRATER
NCG3626
NCG3421
NCG3884
150°
Regulus
165°
NGC3341
Zavijava
Leo
NGC3379
Donebola
11h
12h
Sextans

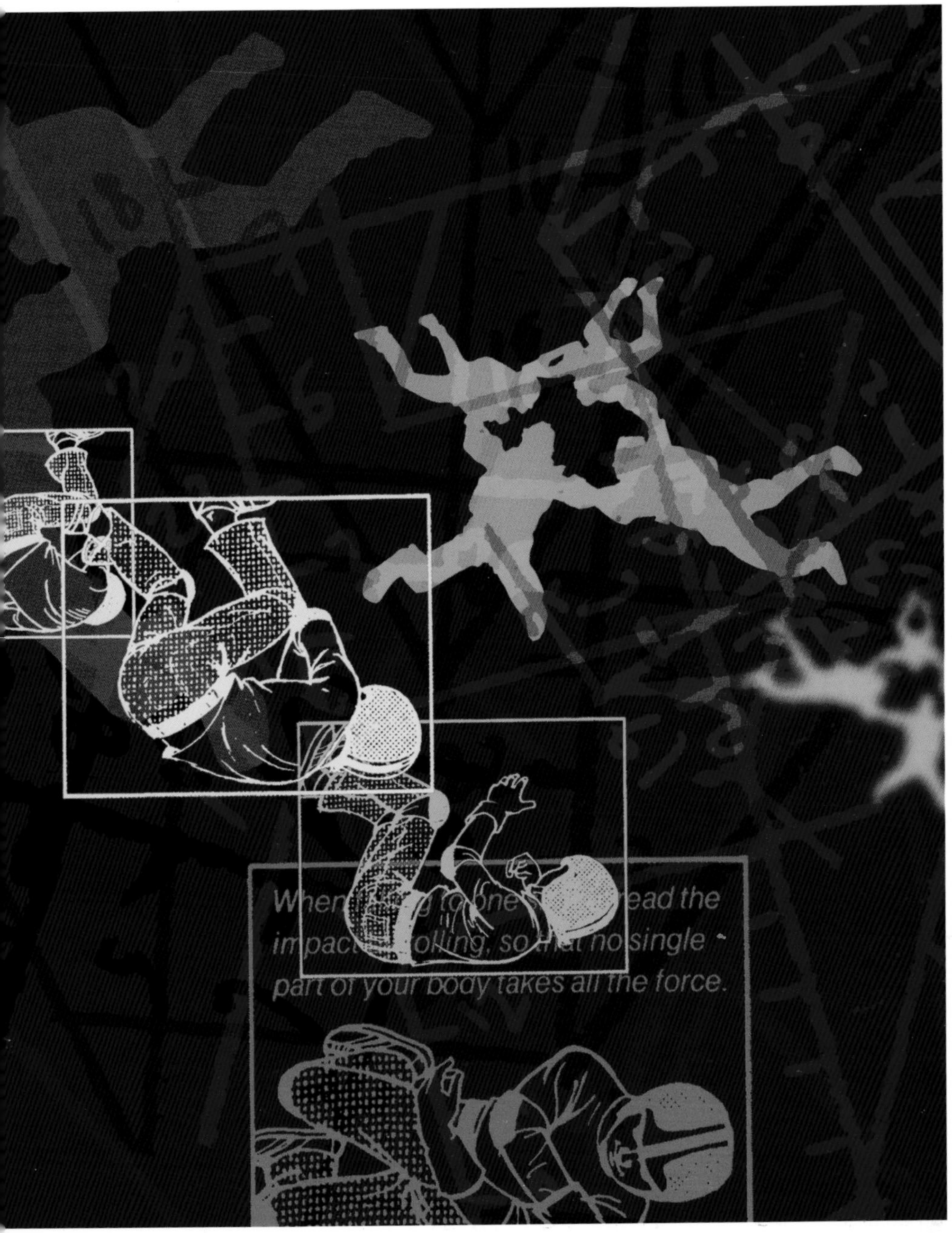
When … to one s… ead the
im pact … olling, so that no single
part of your body takes all the force.

bump

AUG 9TH 1999

EMPLOYEE
OF THE
MONTH

OLIVER MICHAELS

BUMP ASSOCIATES LTD

pillars of wisdom.

issue 7, December 1999, cover photo by Justine

andreas laeufer

styling: Nadine Sanders
photographer's assistants: Sarah Greenwood + Elise Dumontet
thanks to: Ozan

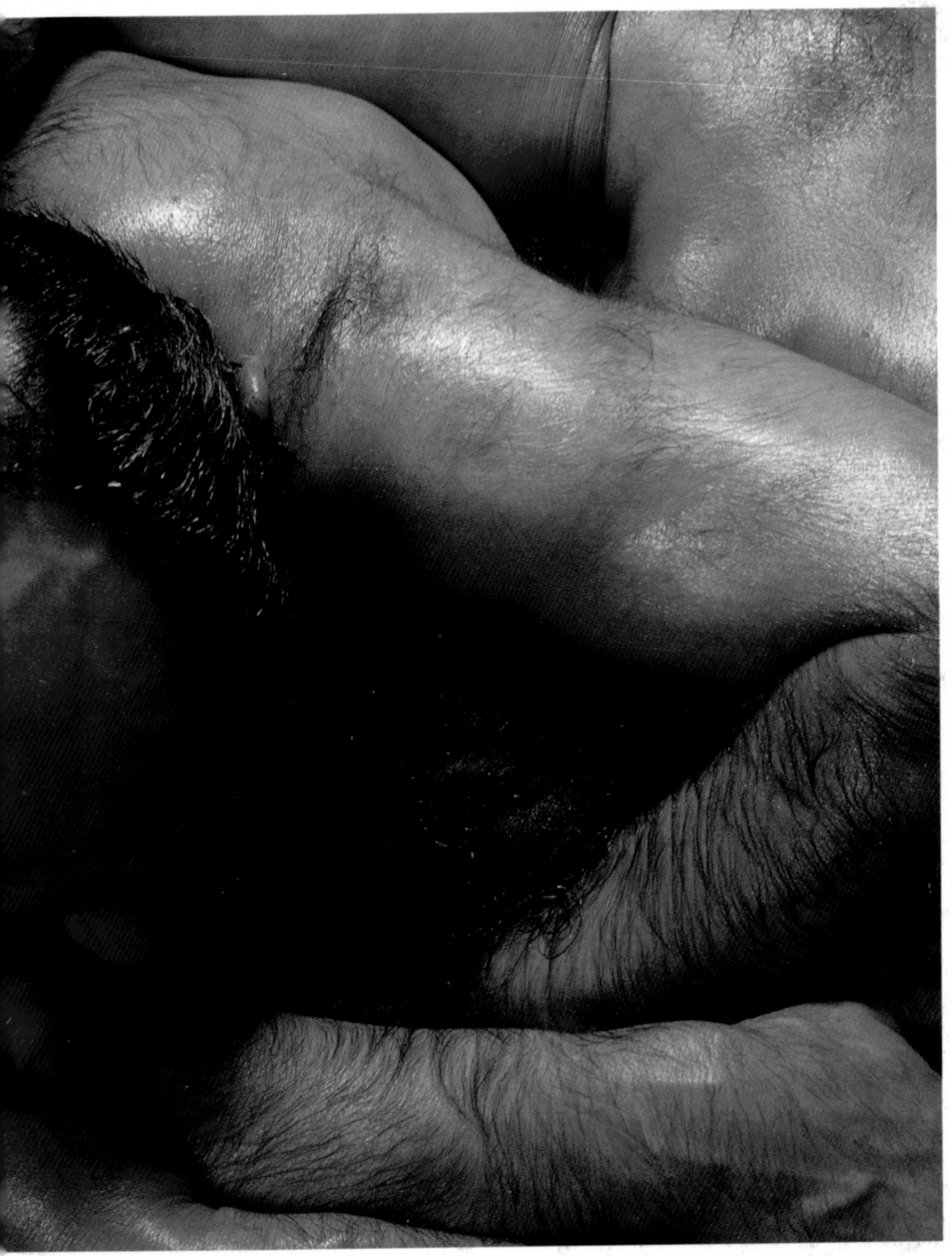

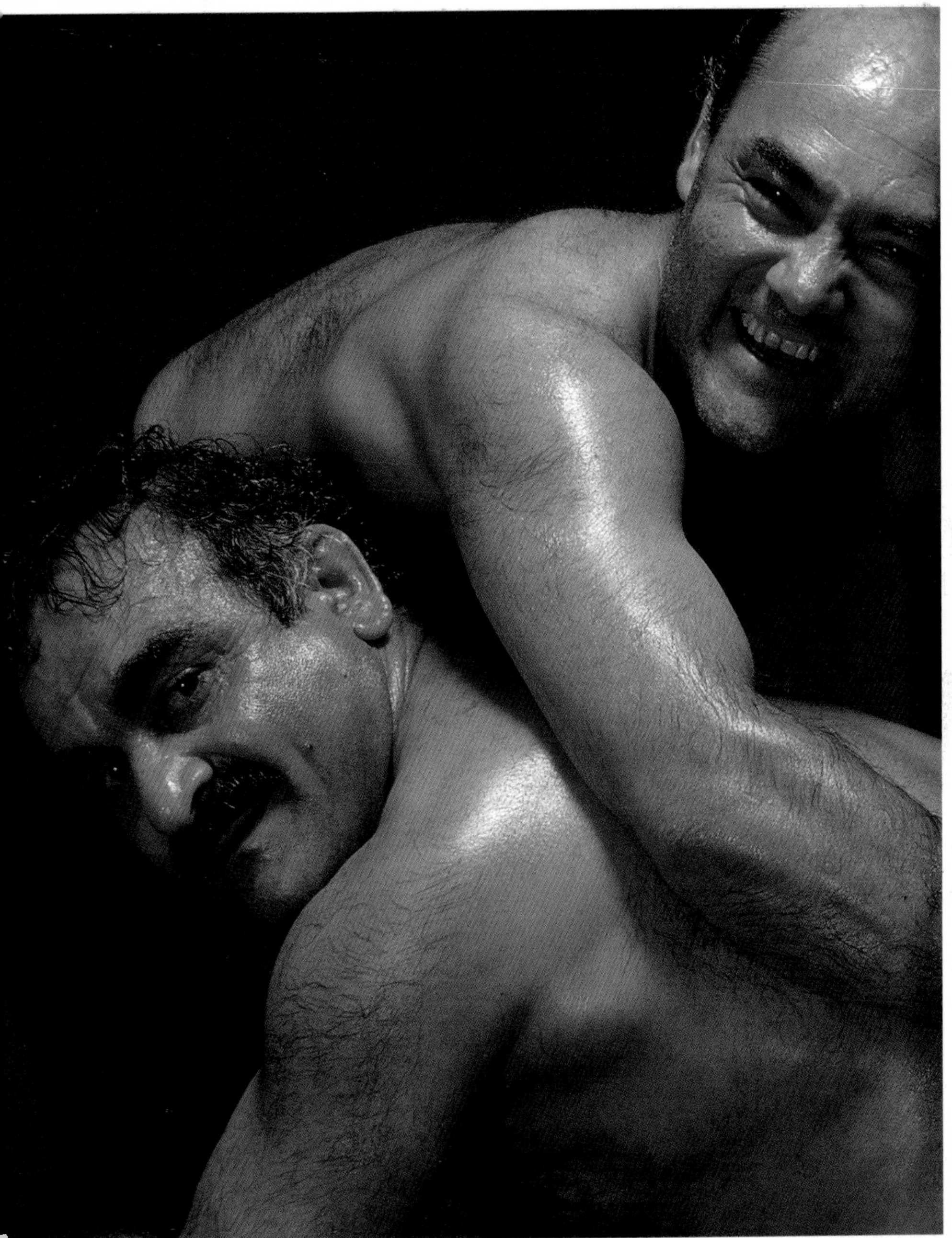

chant
avedissian

CHANT AVEDISSIAN · LE CAIRE

فاروق الأول

julia mckay

styling: Aaron Collins
make-up: Natsuka Yamamoto
hair: Greg Morgan
set/prop design: Adrian Kirby
models: Nick @ Take 2 + Bijan @ Models 1

بسم الله الرحمن الرحيم
الحمد لله رب العالمين الرحمن الرحيم
ملك يوم الدين إياك نعبد وإياك نستعين
اهدنا الصرط المستقيم صرط الذين أنعمت
عليهم غير المغضوب عليهم ولا الضالين

justine

styling: Faye Sawyer
make-up: Nicole Jaritz
hair: Thomas Dunkin
models: Agatha + James Coffee @ Storm

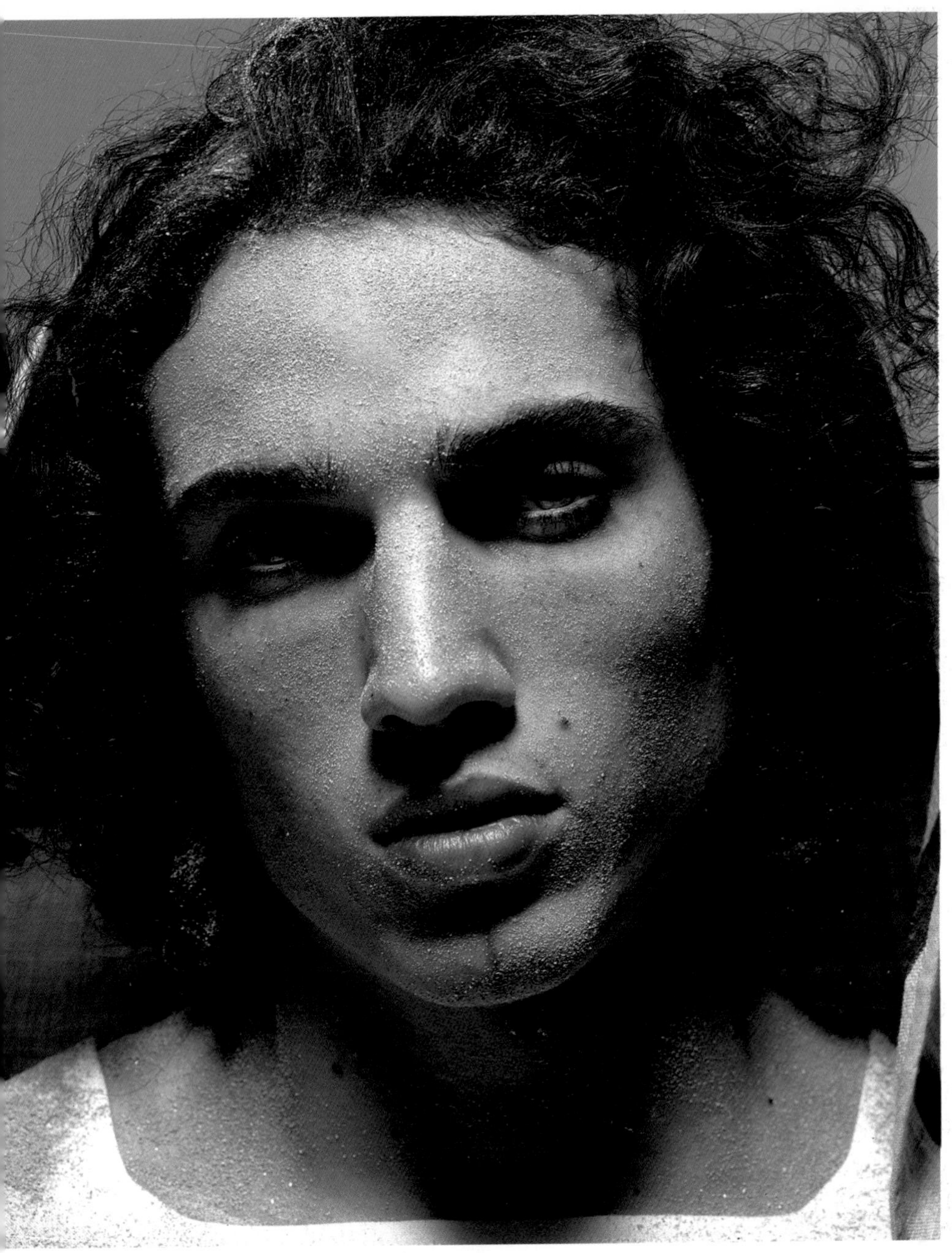

khosrow hassanzadeh

sacha teulon + stacey williams

hair: Asashi
make-up: Neusa
models: Karina @ Take 2 · Aude @ IMG · Frances @ Assassin

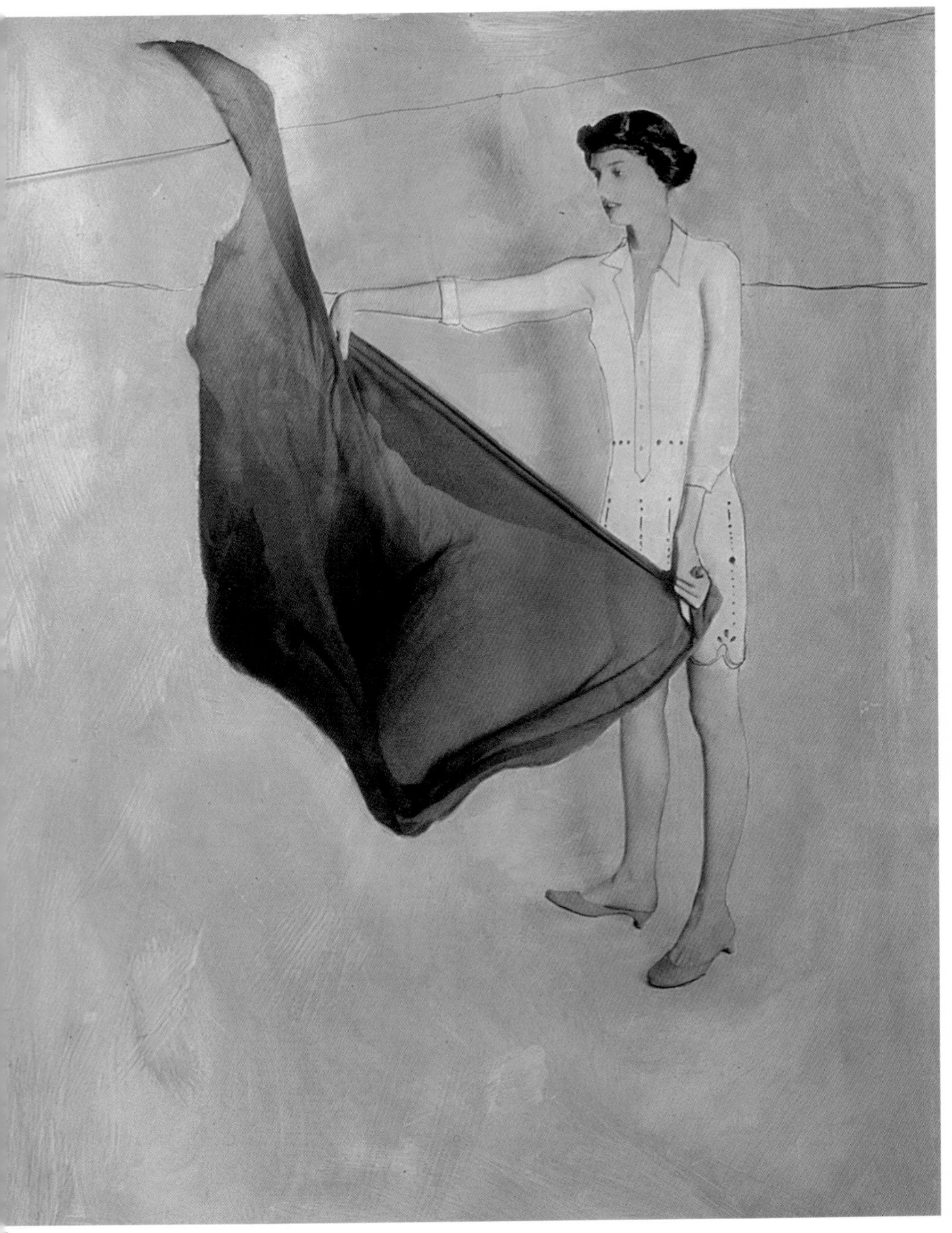

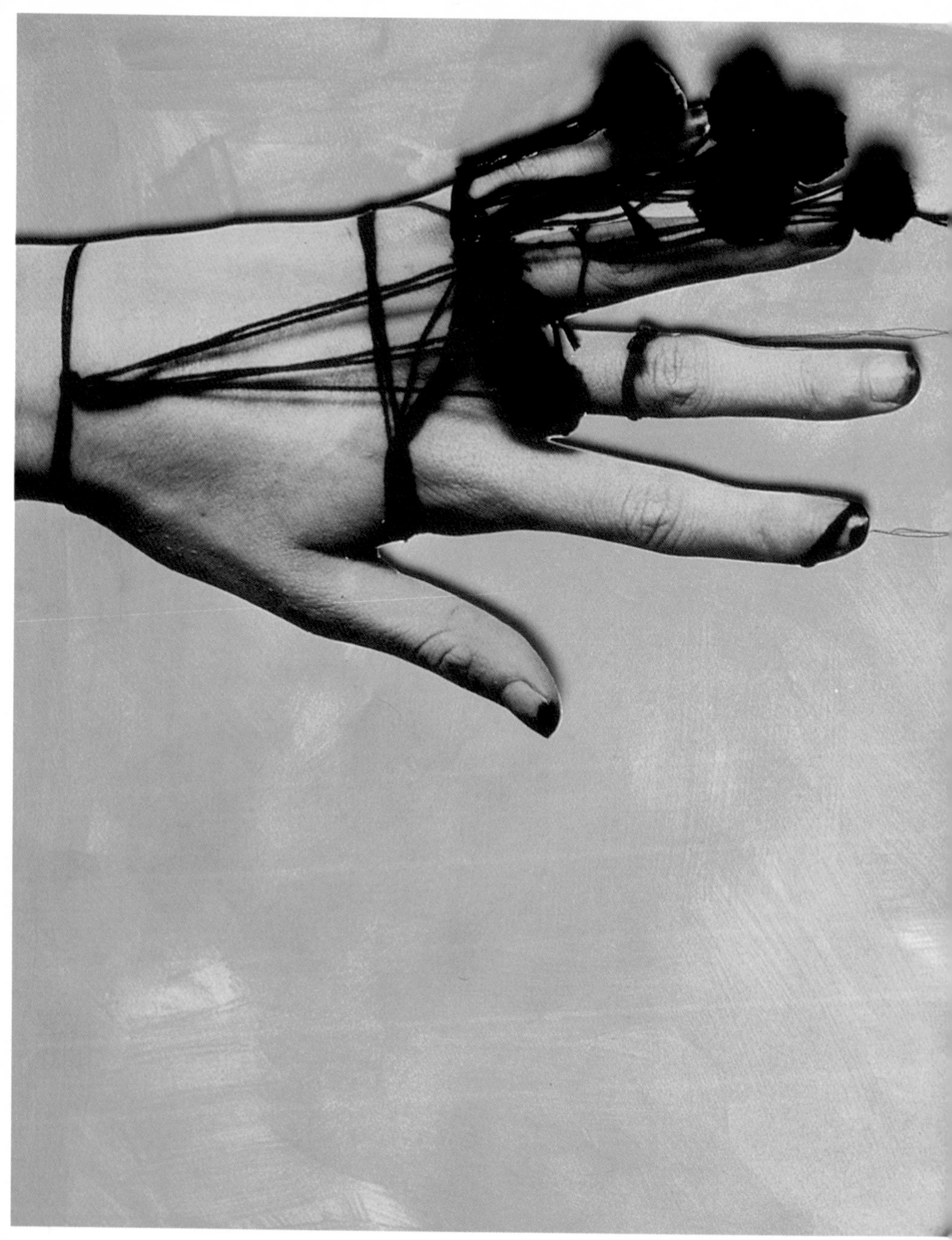

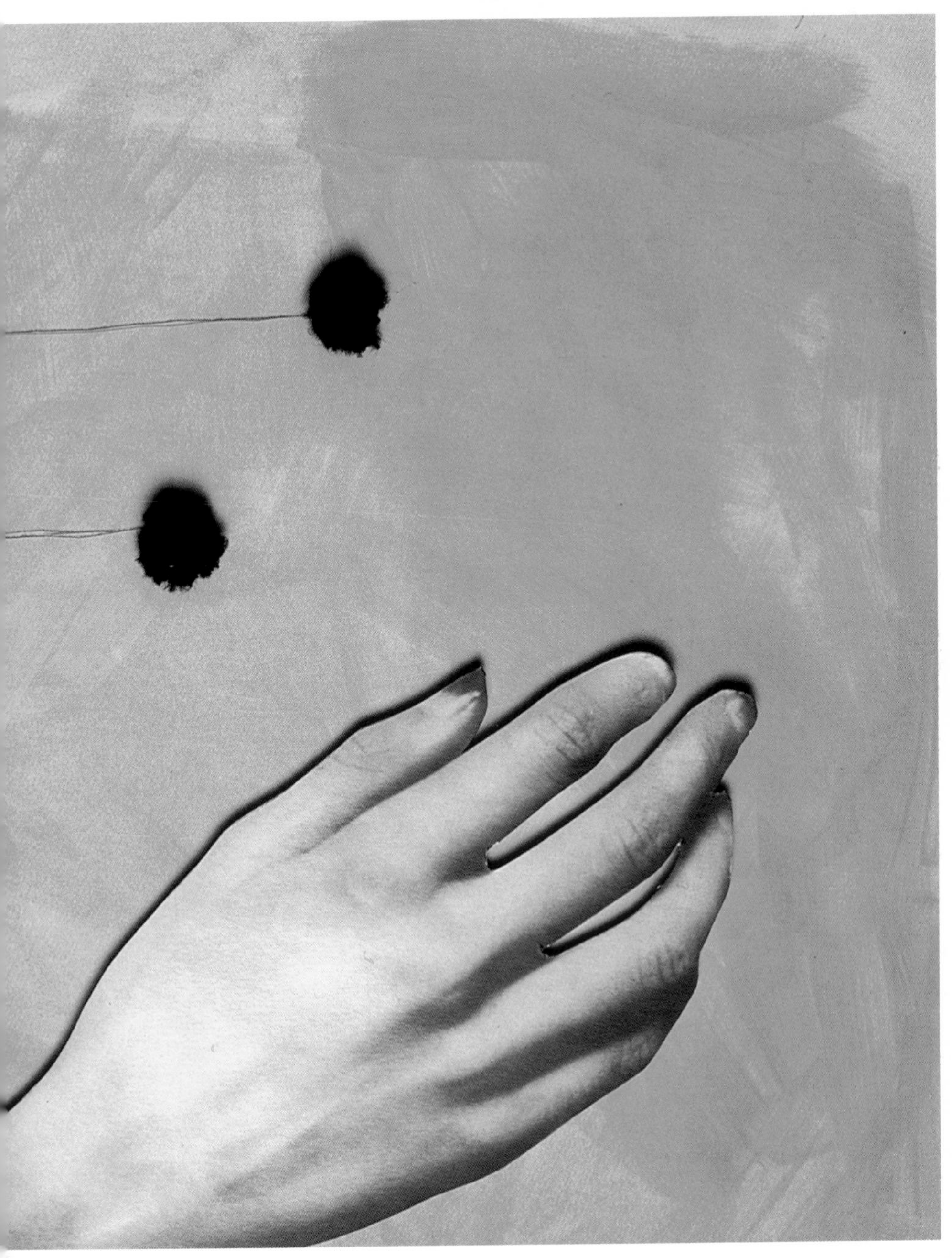

shadi faridian

felix lammers

styling: Mirsaine Lembert
hair: Wendy Jles
make-up + concept: Yasmin Heinz
models: Lynda · Adel · Chaïr · Baharé · Blandine · Nabil

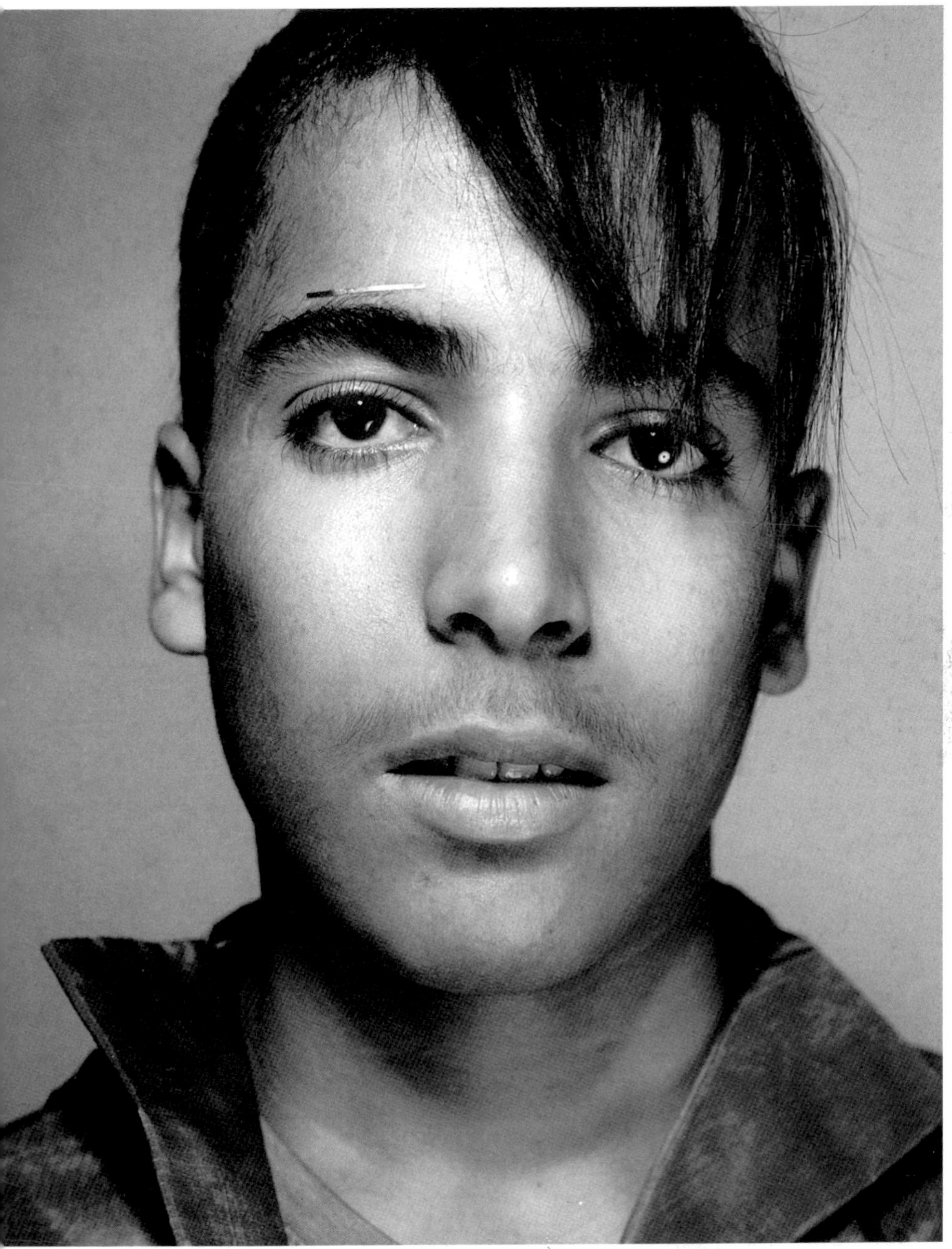

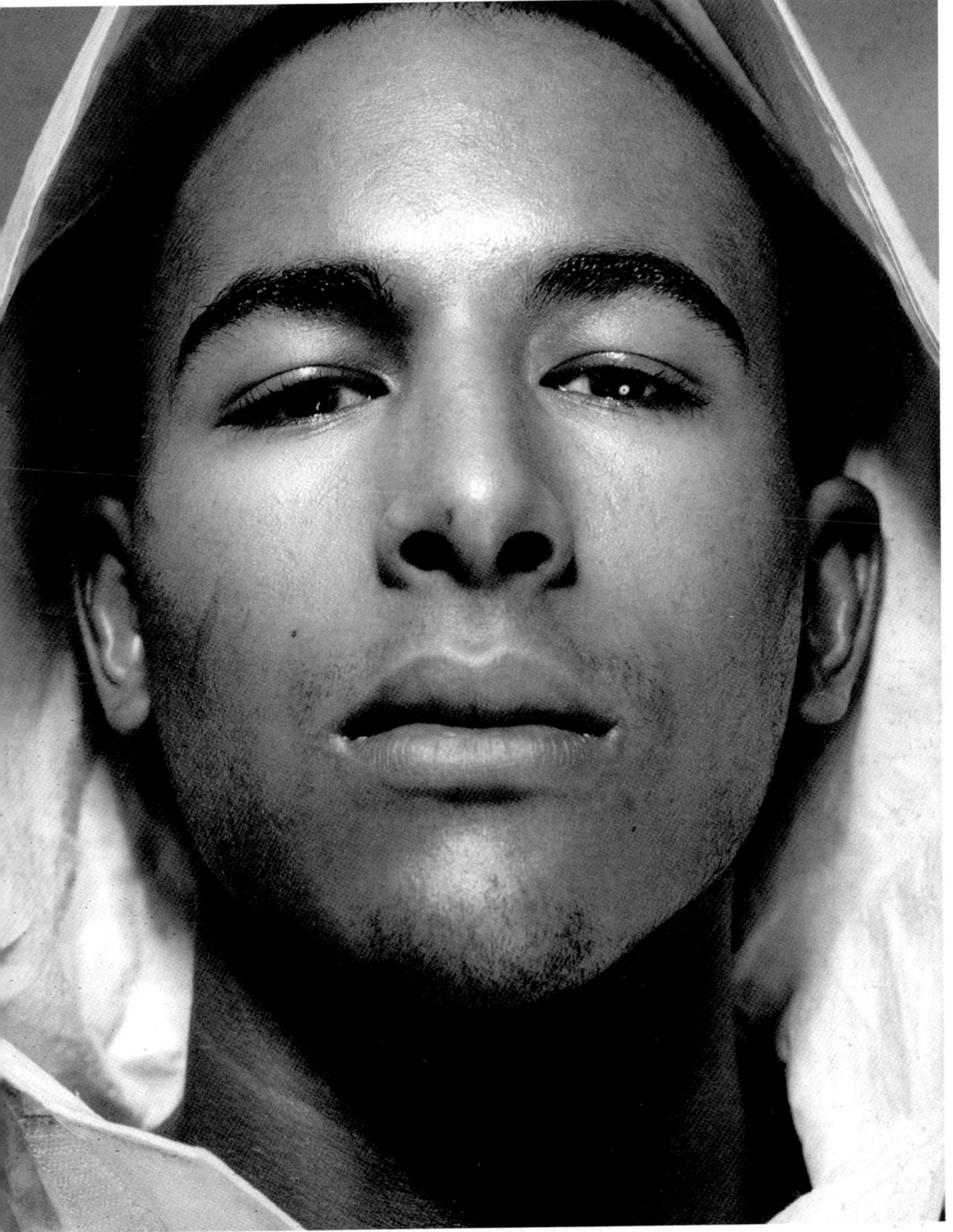

flower powered.

issue 8, February 2000, cover photo by Masoud

anne weatherby

February 2000

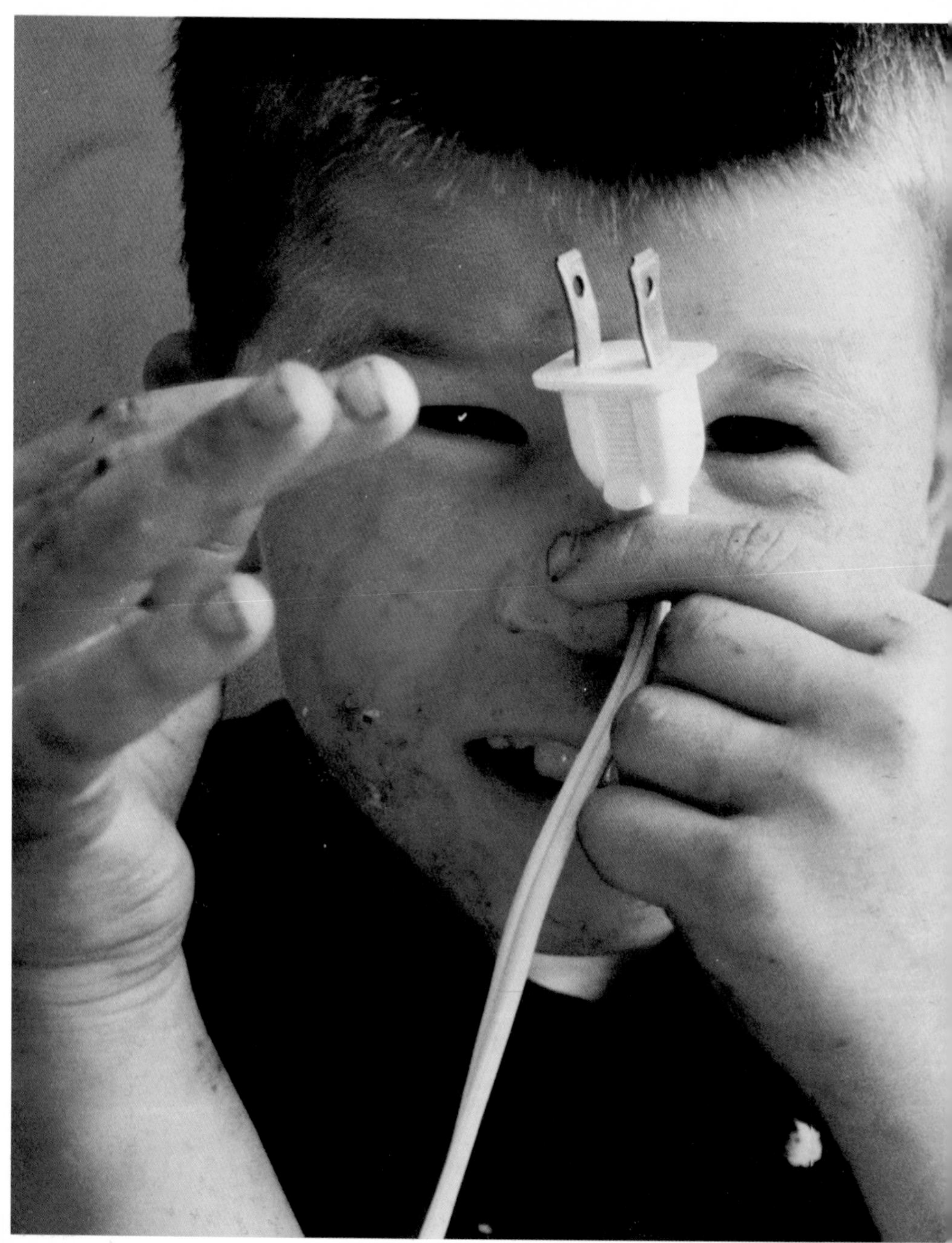

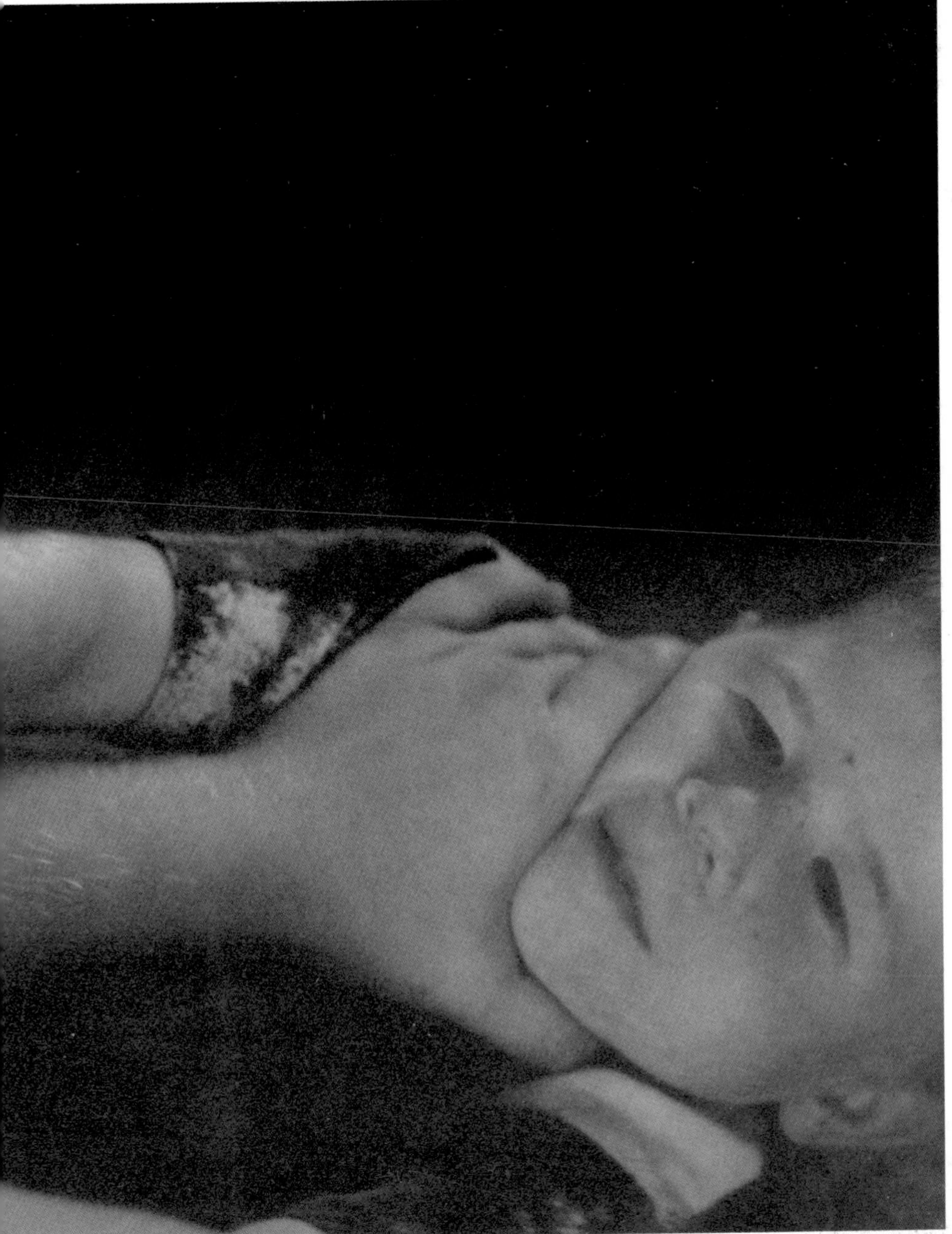

glauce cerveira

@ Danielle Arnaud Gallery, London

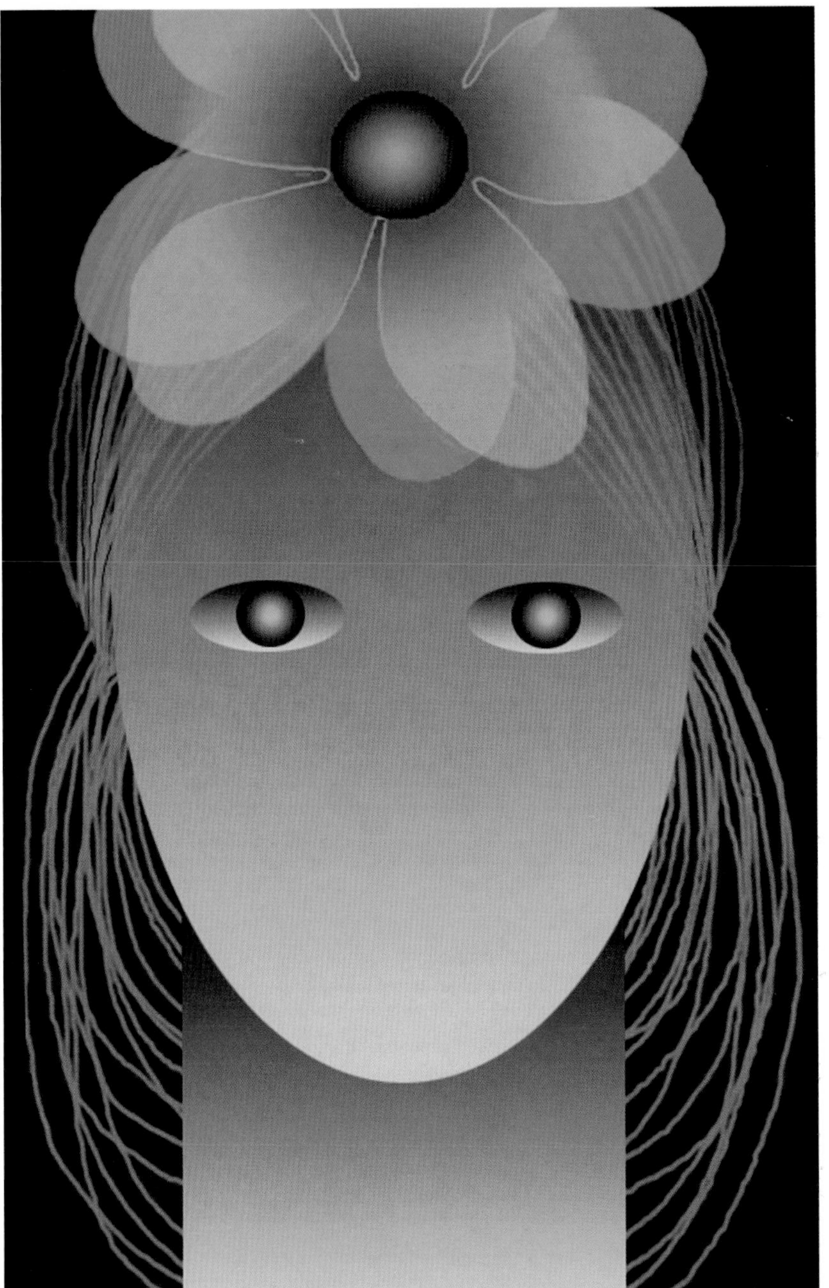

jessica hilltout

February 2000

margaret salmon + dean wiand

February 2000

$500
REWARD
For the Arrest
and Conviction of
JESSE JAMES
HIRAM SIBLEY & CO.
SEEDS

NORTH
AMERICA

BATTSON D. BELFRY
MAYOR

michael danner

February 2000

野生サル注意
危

TOYOTA
ISUZU
CANTER

50
50
VOICE
Deliboy

nick
pearce

February 2000

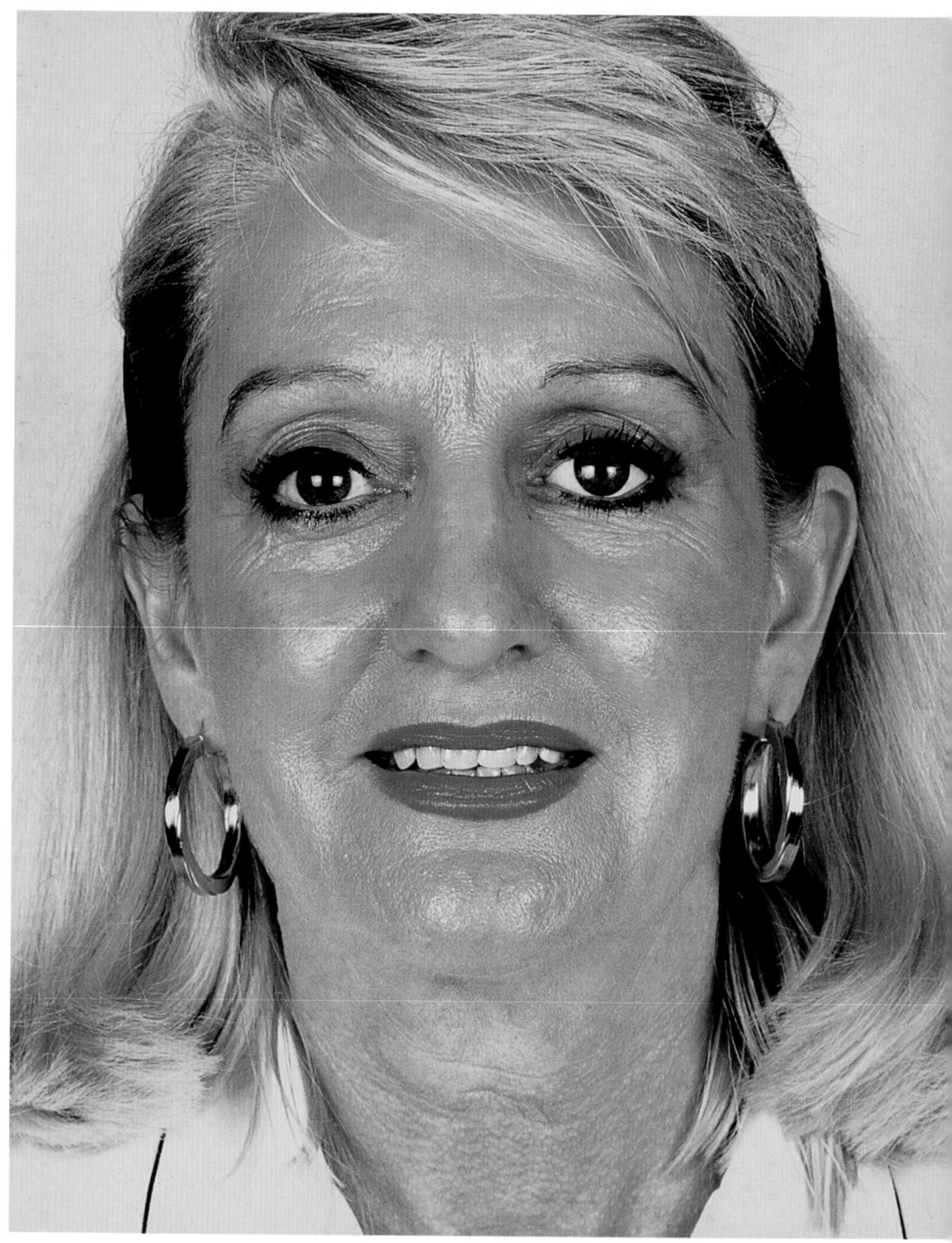

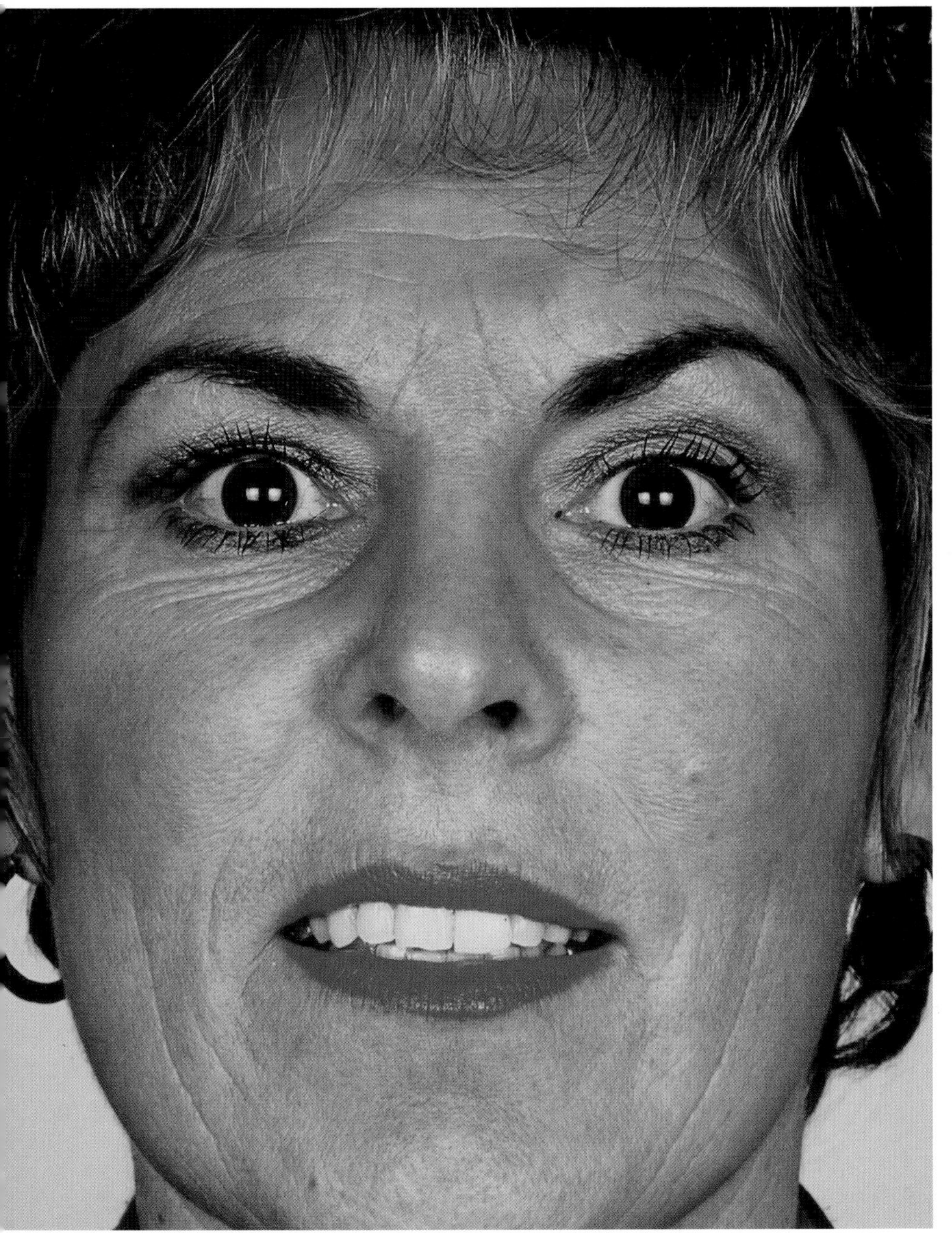

piet
paris

February 2000

DAY 1

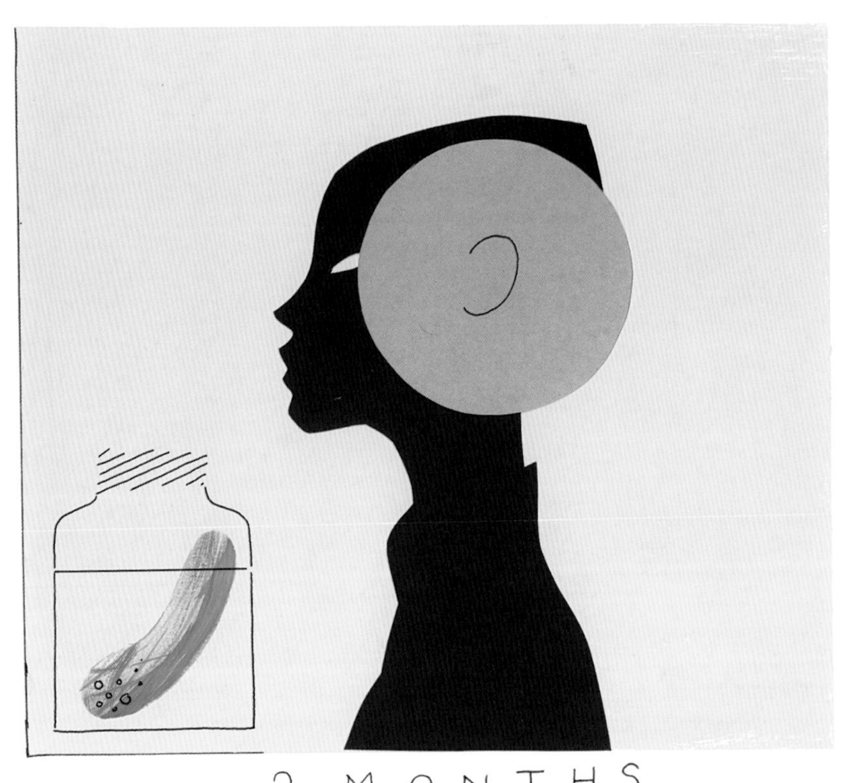

2 MONTHS

4 MONTHS

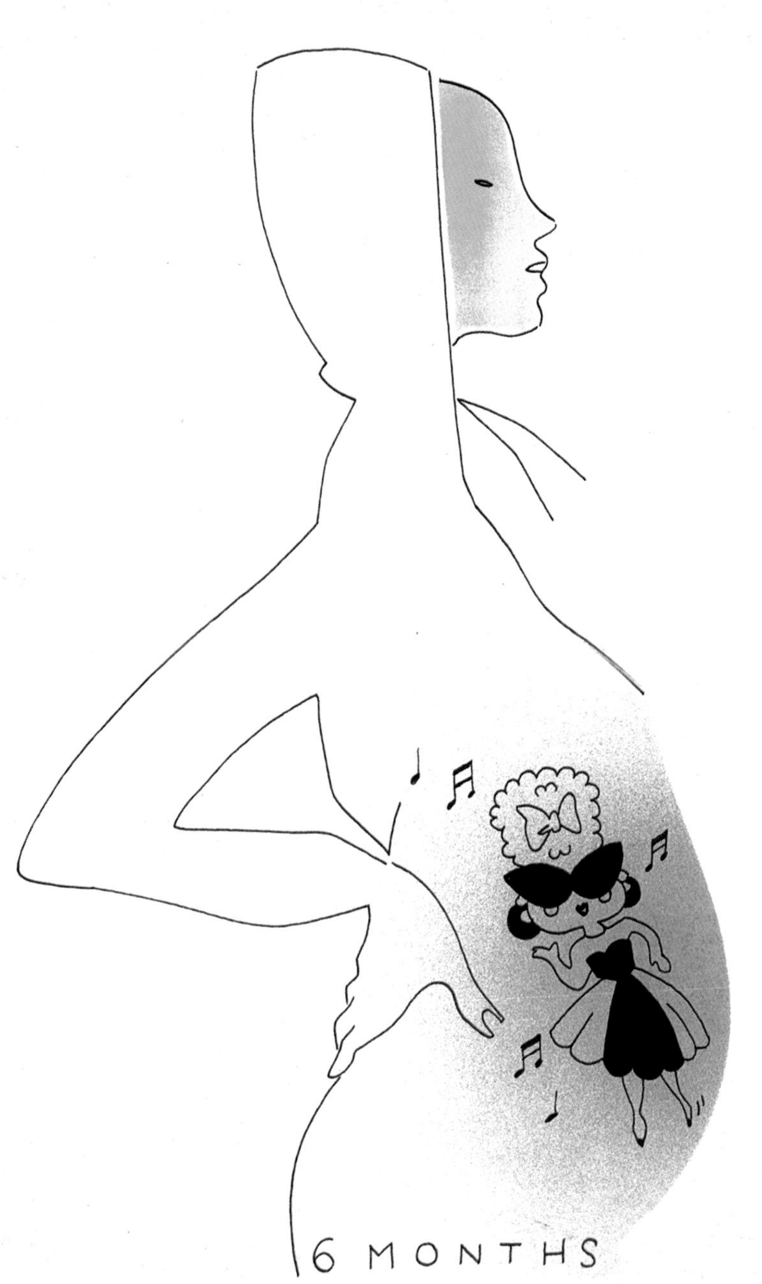
6 MONTHS

Joanna Kostka

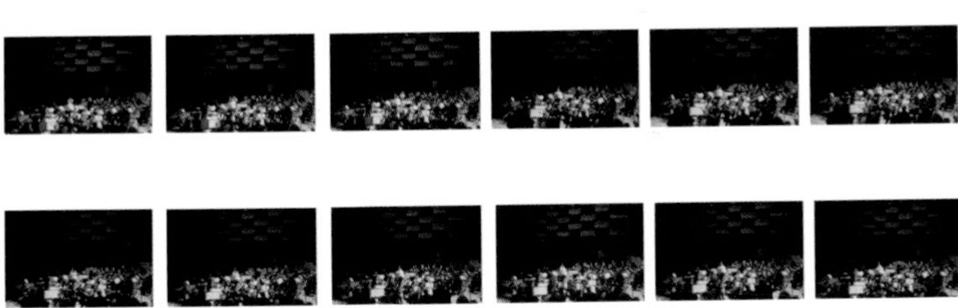

00:00:00

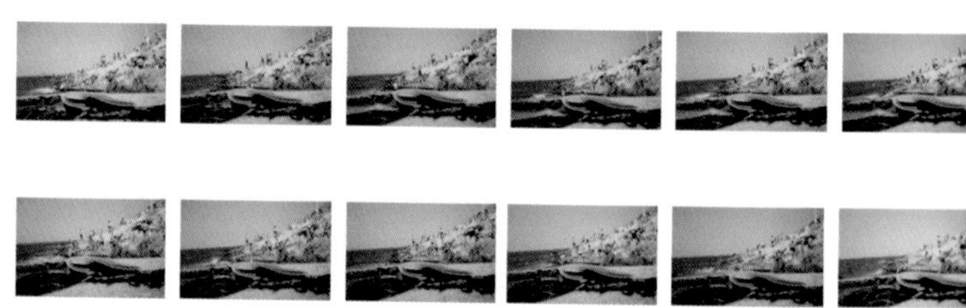

00:01:00

00:00:00

00:00:10

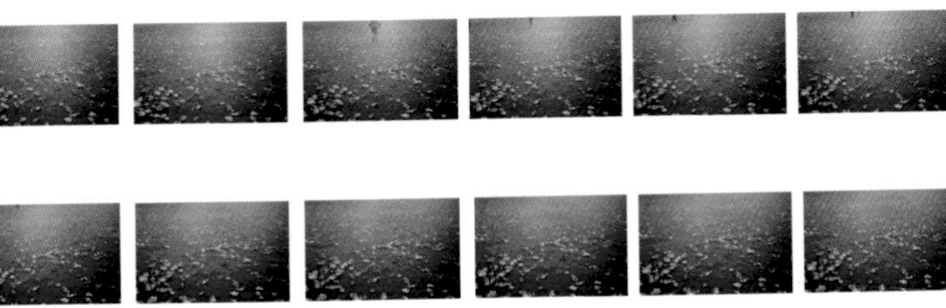

sandro sodano + jo phillips

styling: Jo Phillips
hair: Asashi
make-up: Phillipe Miletto
set design: Adam Dawe
post production: Horacio Herrera Richmond
models: Marie Claire, Kirsten, Marissa

glossy posse.

issue 9, April 2000, cover photo by Sabine Pigalle

bruce gilden

courtesy of Bruce Gilden / Magnum Photos London

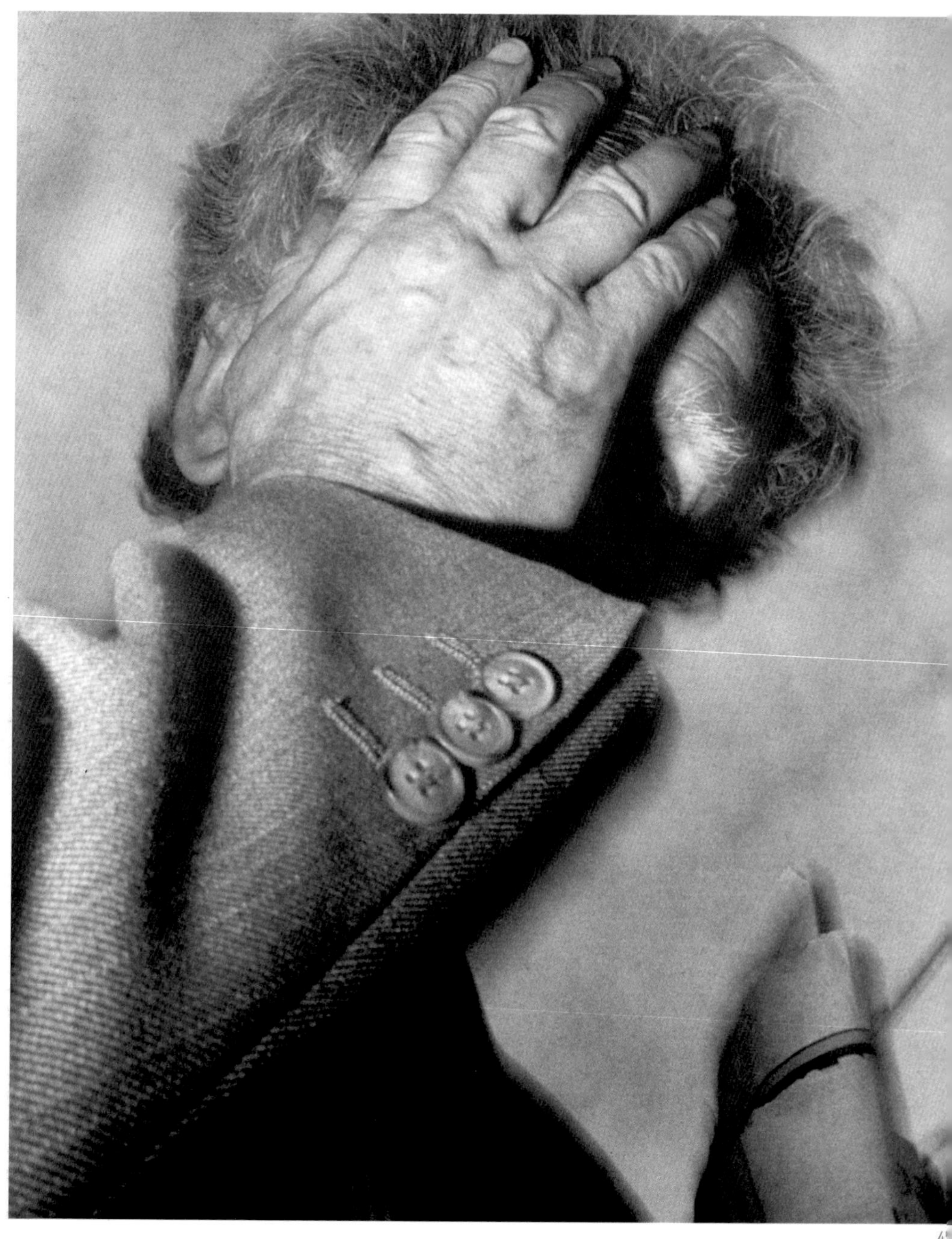

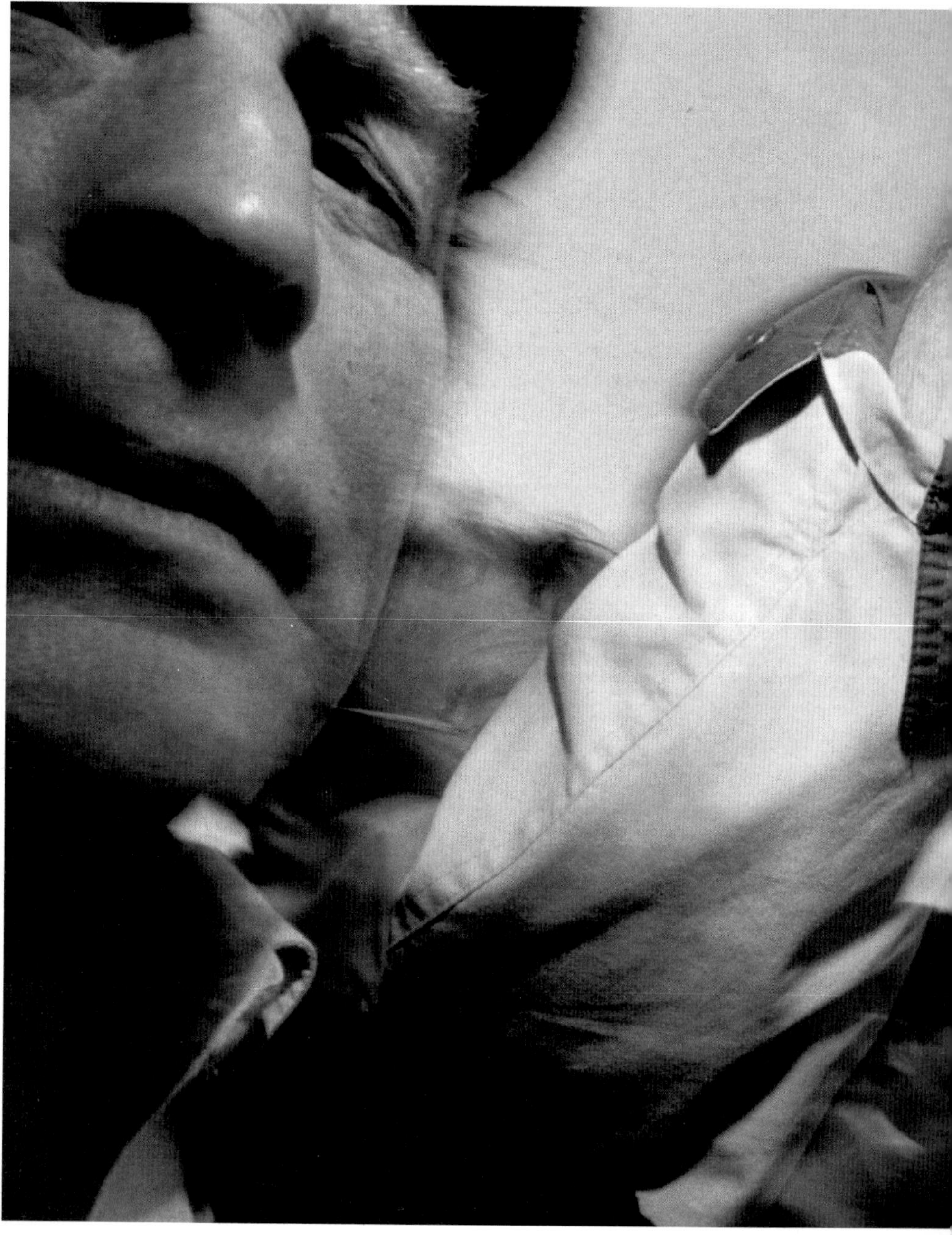

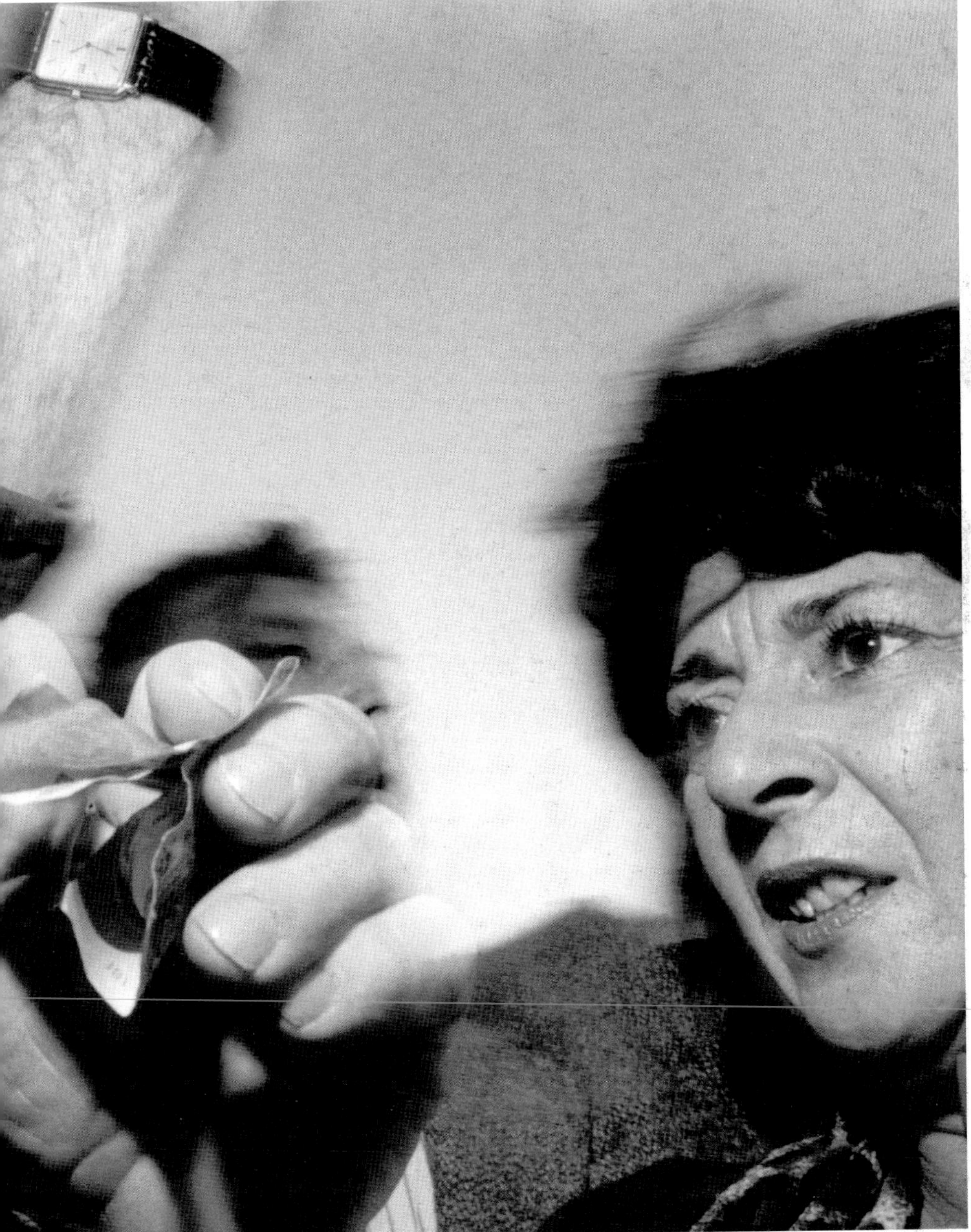

david thorpe

@ Maureen Paley / Interim Art, London

April 2000

stephen gill

April 2000

The Ballad of the Hebrew Slaves, Verdi

Prettty Fly for a White Guy, Offspring

Love Me Tender, Elvis Presley

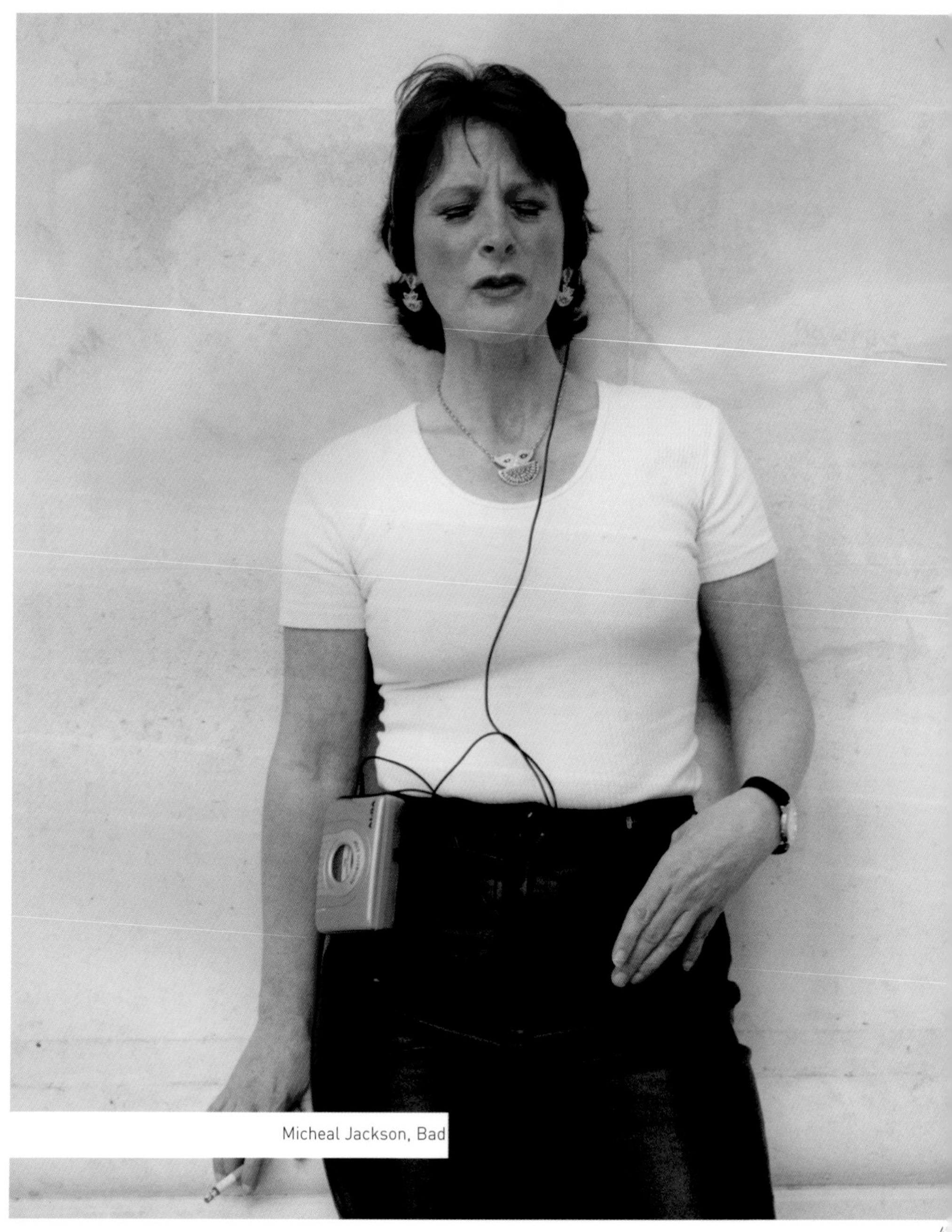

Micheal Jackson, Bad

Back to the 60's

gyslain yarhi

styling: Virginie Dhello
make-up: Isabelle Jonieaux
hair: Philipinne Cardan
model: Milena @ Nathalie

per hüttner

April 2000

CONTACT
4800431
6460633

ZIEDI
DANA1
DN 277
CH-6053

martin parr

courtesy of Martin Parr / Magnum Photos London + Phaidon Press

jean-pierre khazem

@ Galerie Emmanuel Perrotin, Paris

Be complices

complices?

complices
complices , happy , fresh ,

sabine pigalle

styling: Christophe Martinez
hair: Maxime Massé
make-up: Huê-Lan Van Duc
models: Kari-Anne @ Next + Diana @ Marylin

April 2000

lee powers

styling: Cynthia Lawrence-John
hair: George Ng-Yu-Tin
make-up: John Christopher
models: Adeola @ Models 1 · Lulla + Michelle @ Select · Nina + Emma @ IMG

<u>HAVE YOU SEEN</u>

our super lovers skirt
and seraph shirt. they are young and
vulnerable. there is a loving home and
family waiting for them. they were last
seen in the covent garden area. if you
have any information however small
please contact us or the police. just
let us know they are safe.

tel: 0117 - 862 - 11901 ask for pat.

Missing and Missed
Have you seen Annette Huitzsch. Our beloved is missing. Have you seen her?
Pink with red spots. Please help us and telephone if you see her.
Jo- 07667- 362 964z

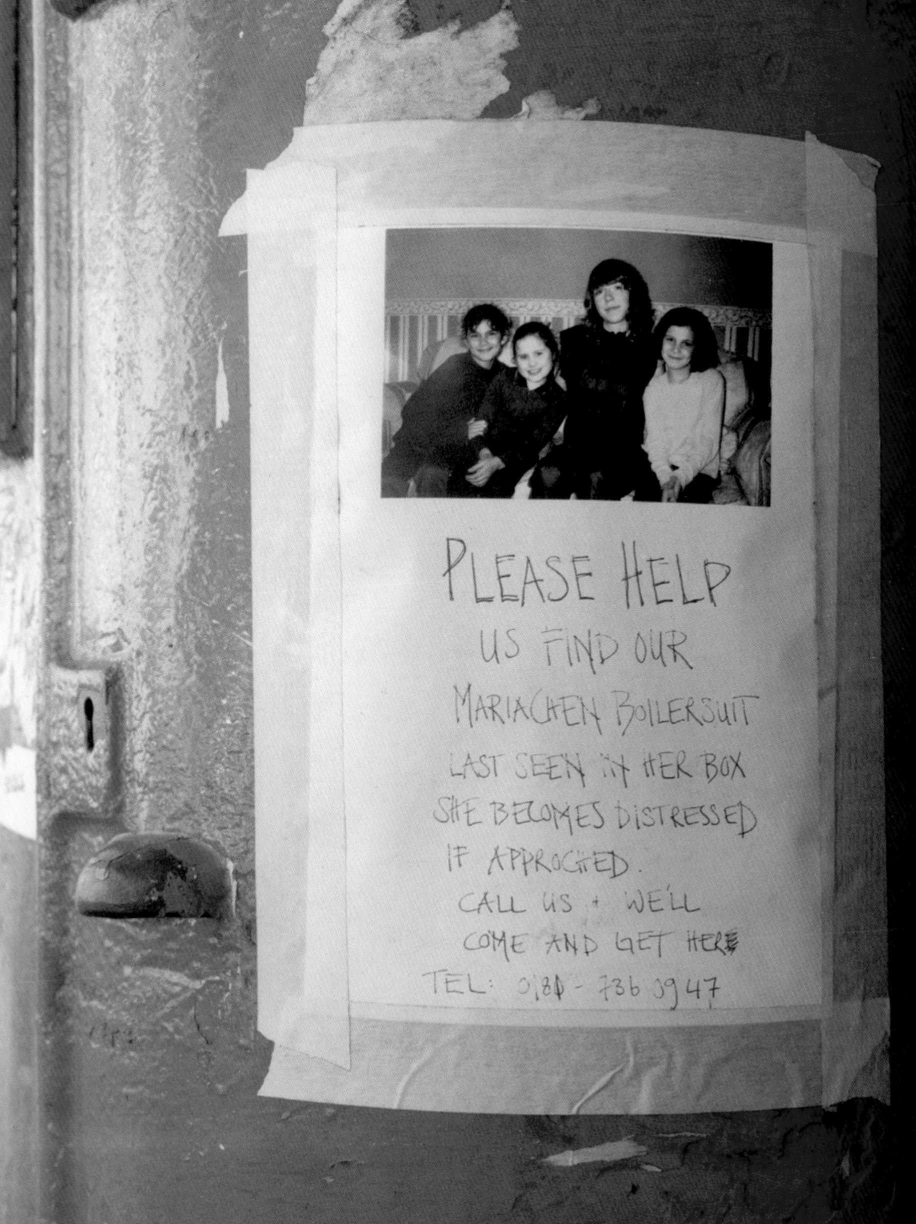
PLEASE HELP
US FIND OUR
MARIACHEN BOILERSUIT
LAST SEEN IN HER BOX
SHE BECOMES DISTRESSED
IF APPROCHED.
CALL US + WE'LL
COME AND GET HERE
TEL: 0181 - 736 0947

thierry van biesen

styling: Marianne Ghantous
hair: Juan-Carlos
make-up: Polly Osmond
models: Lydia K + Jesse Wade @ Select

thomas brun

styling: Lena Ulven

April 2000

furniture for the mind.

issue 10, July 2000, cover photo Kutlu

kate plumb

styling: Victoria Adcock
hair: Lance Lowe
make-up: Hina Dohi
model: Tatyana @ Next

kutlu

make-up: Susan McCarthy

matthieu deluc

styling: Sanaa Djellal
make-up: Stéphanie
hair: Zilia

7

mie takahashi

クロッカー♡
ト大作戦Meeting~
CADE
MAXI SINGLE
ダーリン』
lease!!

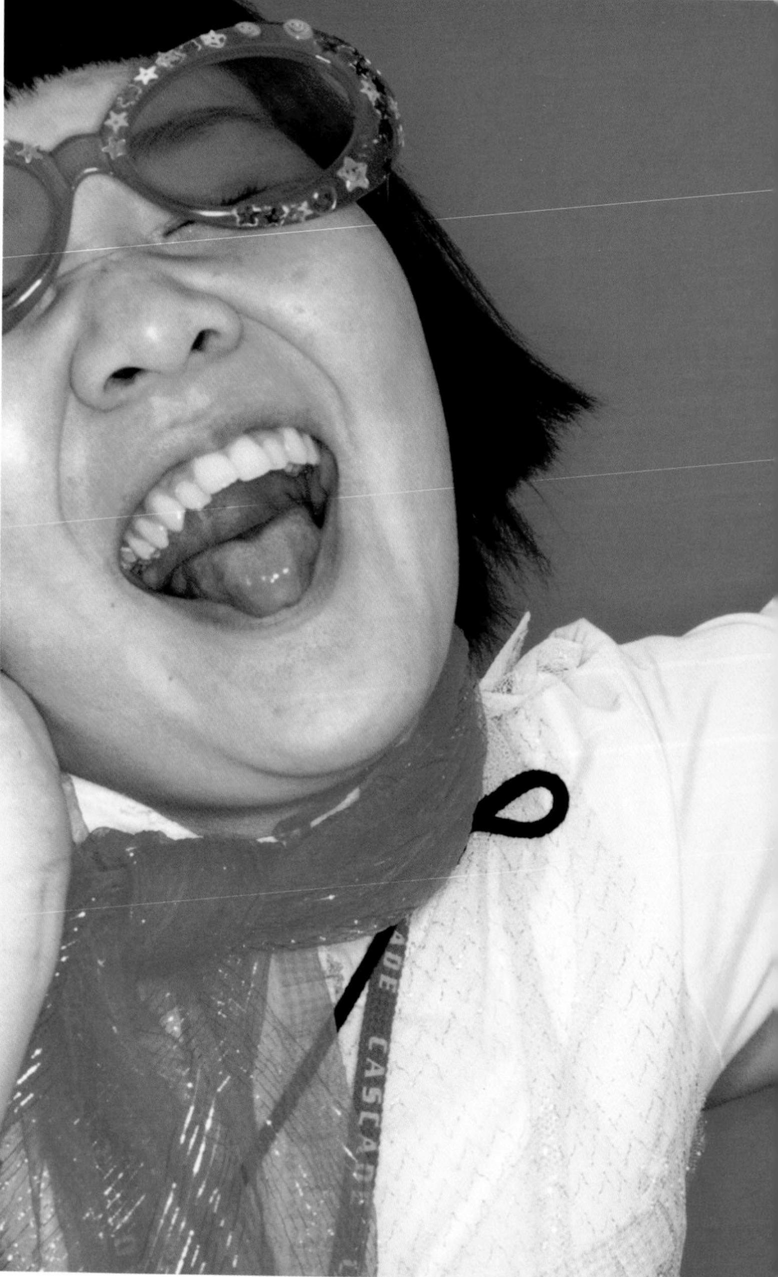
CASCADE

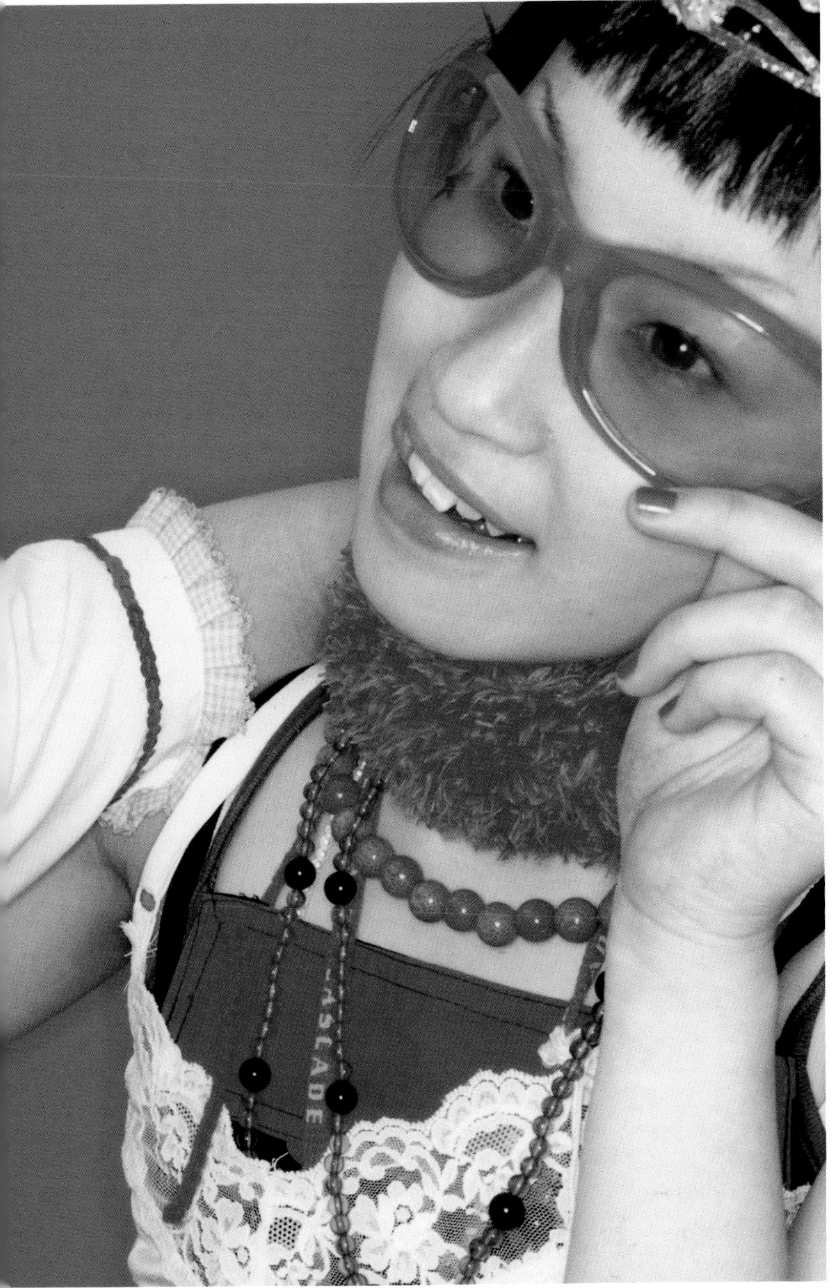

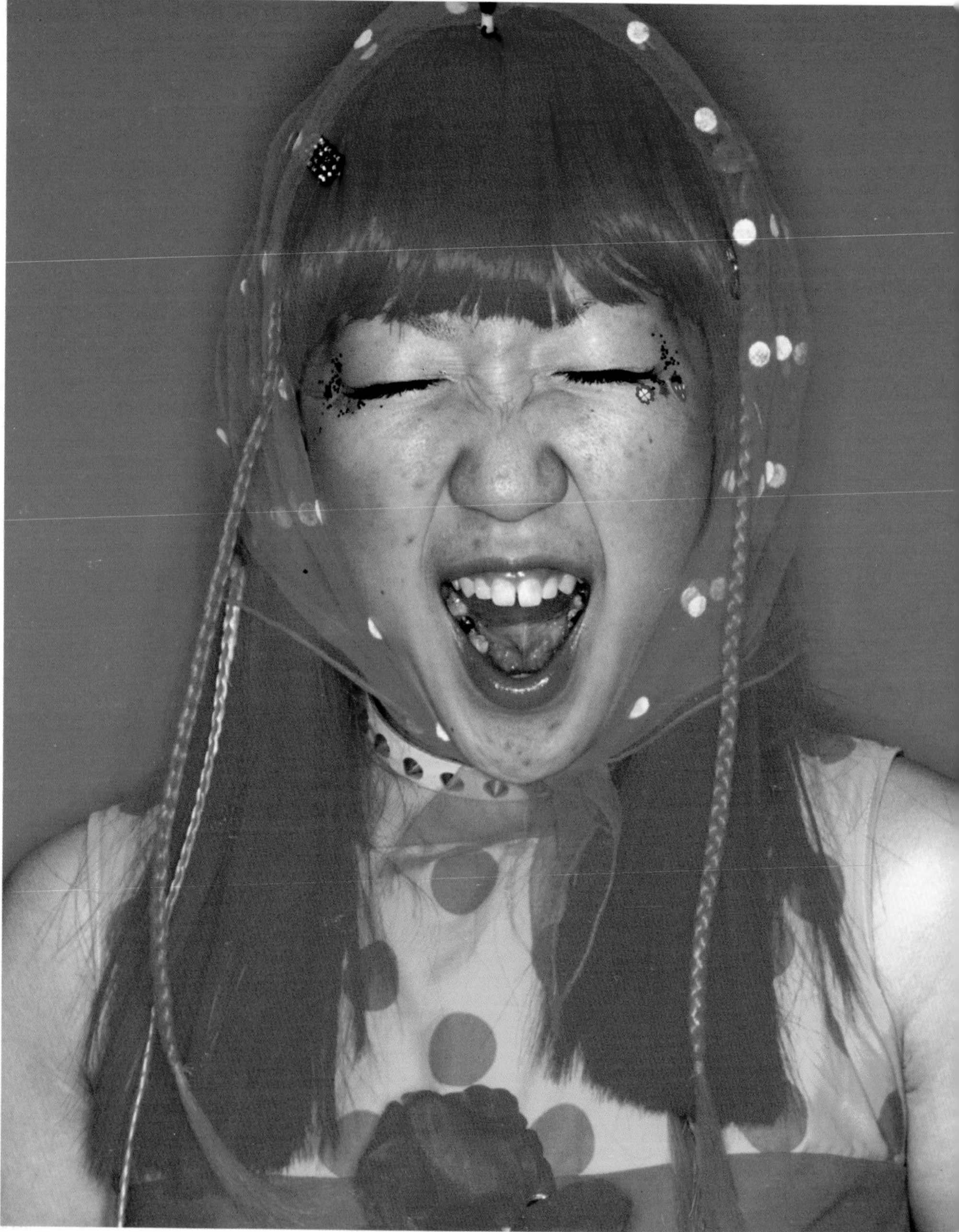

patricia estanguet

styling: Gil Lesage
make-up + hair: Miky
models: Maya + Lou + Penny the dog

RAGILE FRAGILE FRAGILE FR
EROS
FRAGILE
AGILE
AGILE FR
RAGILE FRAGILE F

costes

LOU

greg stogdon

photos: Masoud
styling: Keiko Seya

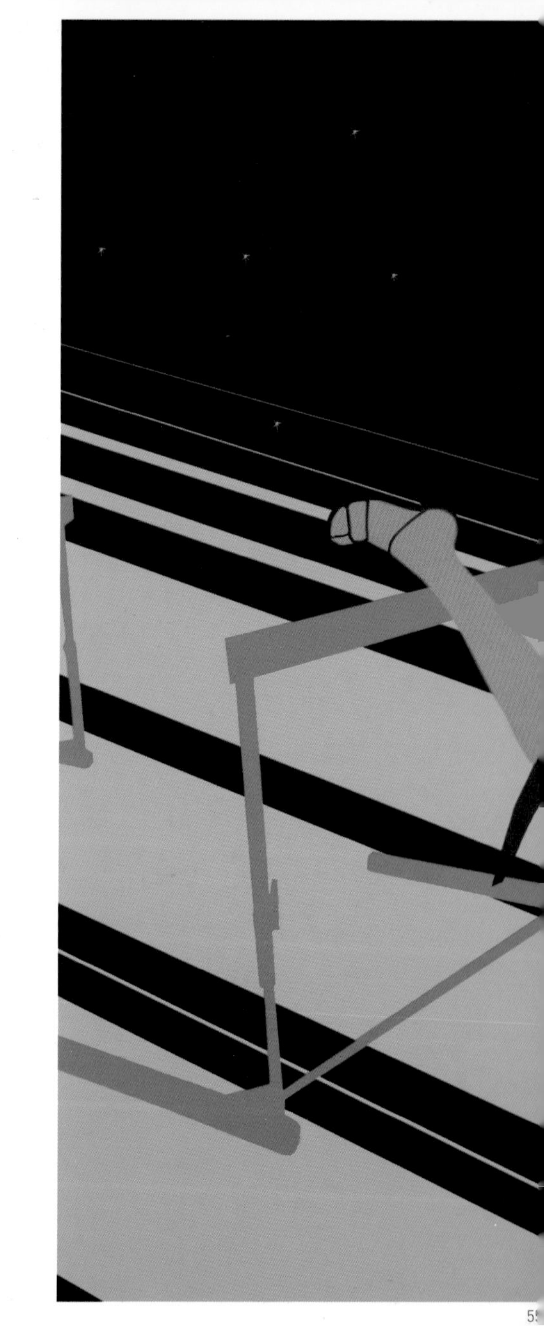

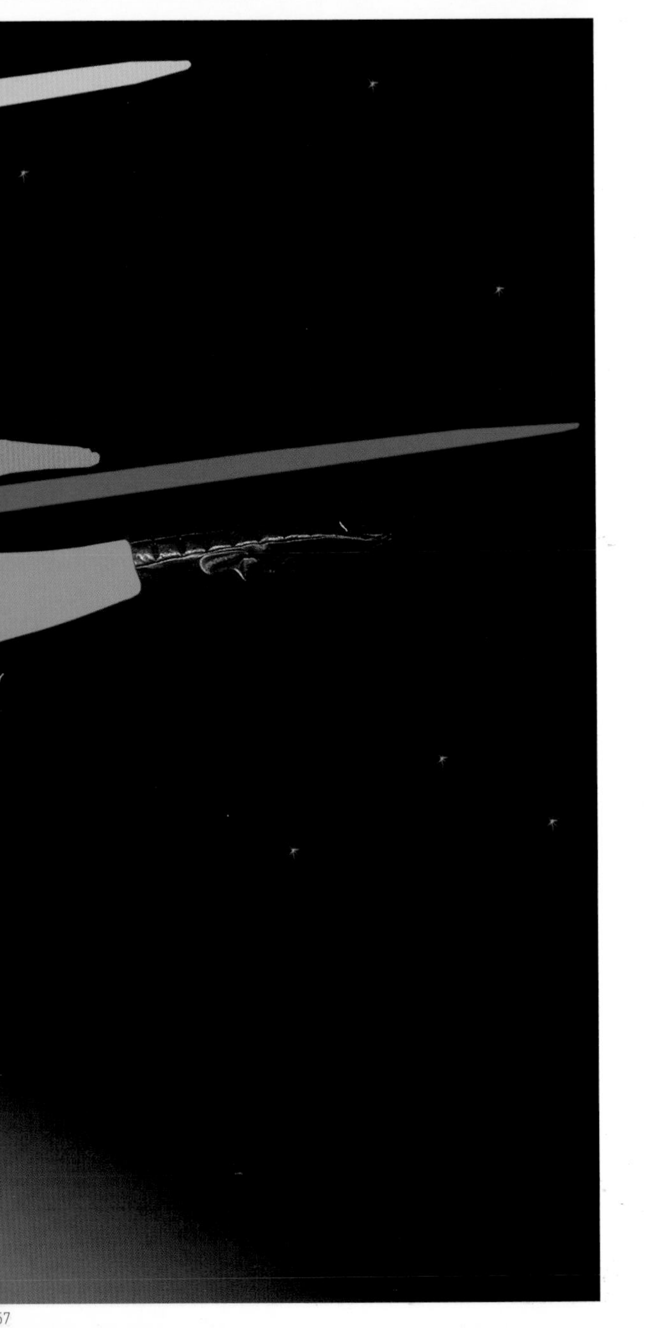

peter benson

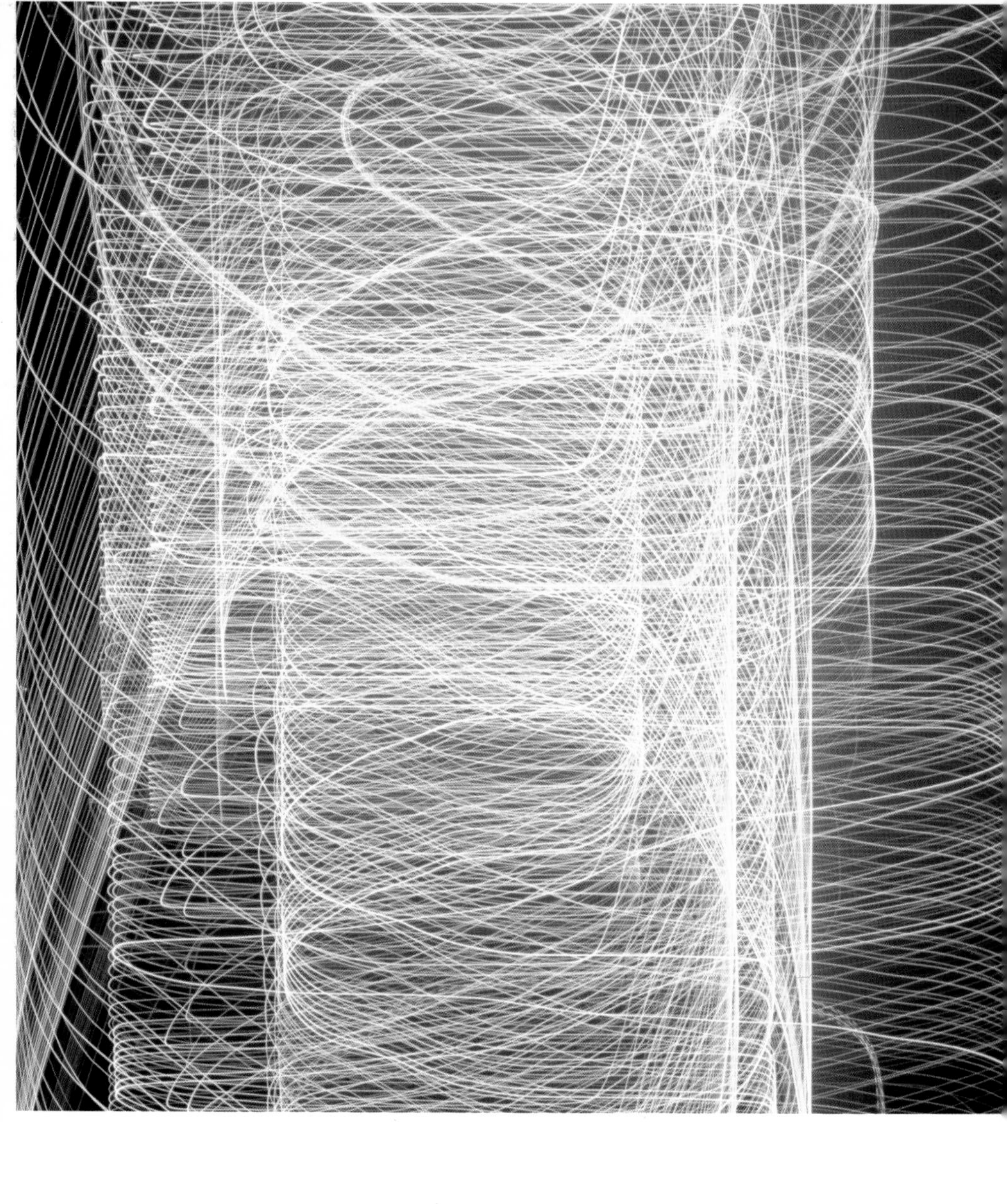

aes
group

علي
رضي الله عنه

C.B.U.
الرحمن الرحيم

R GUGGENHEIM MUSEUM

freeborn,
free based,
free be.

issue 11, September 2000, cover photo by Felix Lammers

anne deniau

styling: Aurélie Lambillon
hair: Becky Dobney
make-up: Adam de Cruz
models: Natasha Prince @ Storm · Ursa + Bianca @ Next

No culture

No creation

No respect

No reality

No chic

dominik gigler

styling: Juliane Kahl
model: Otto Glueck

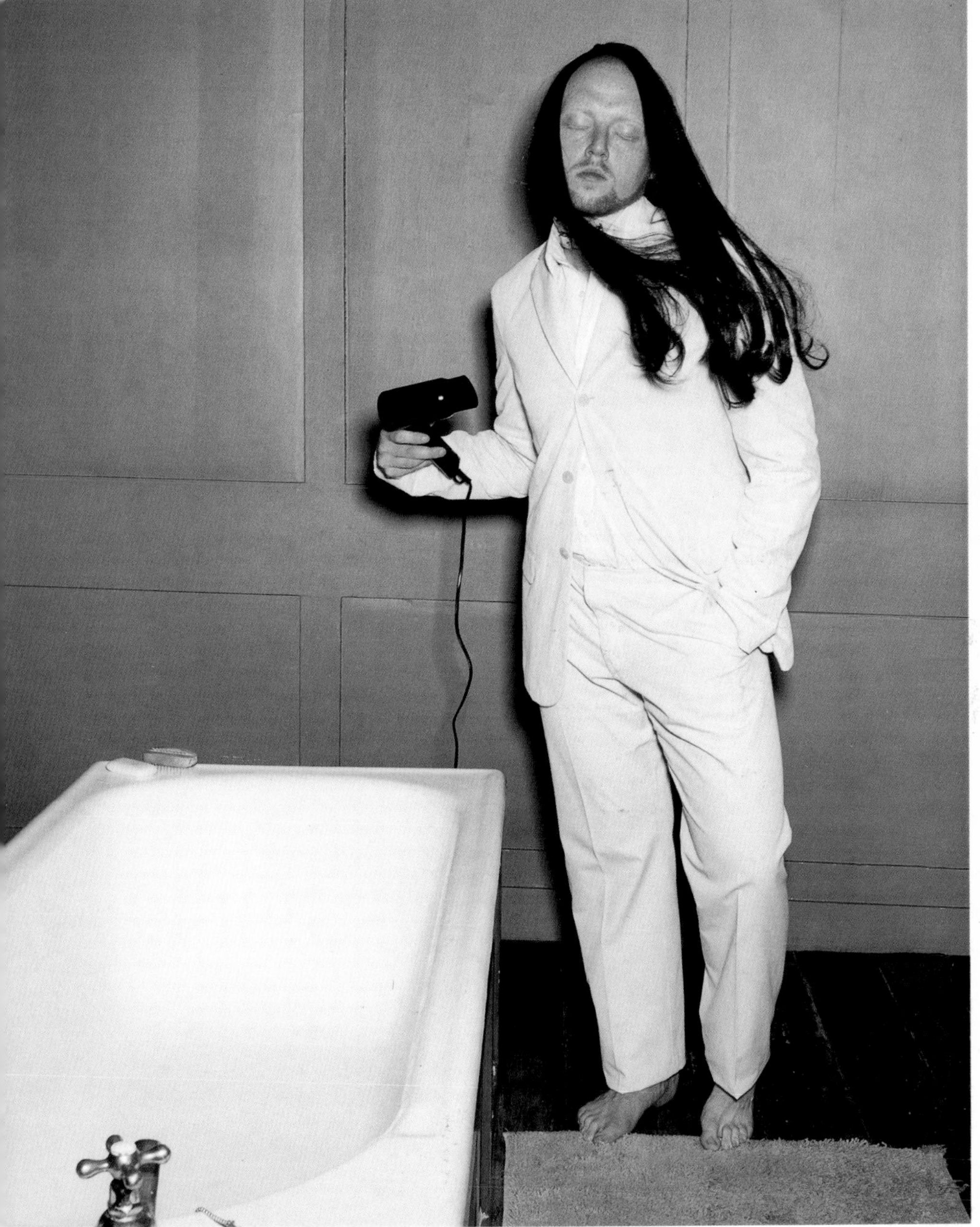

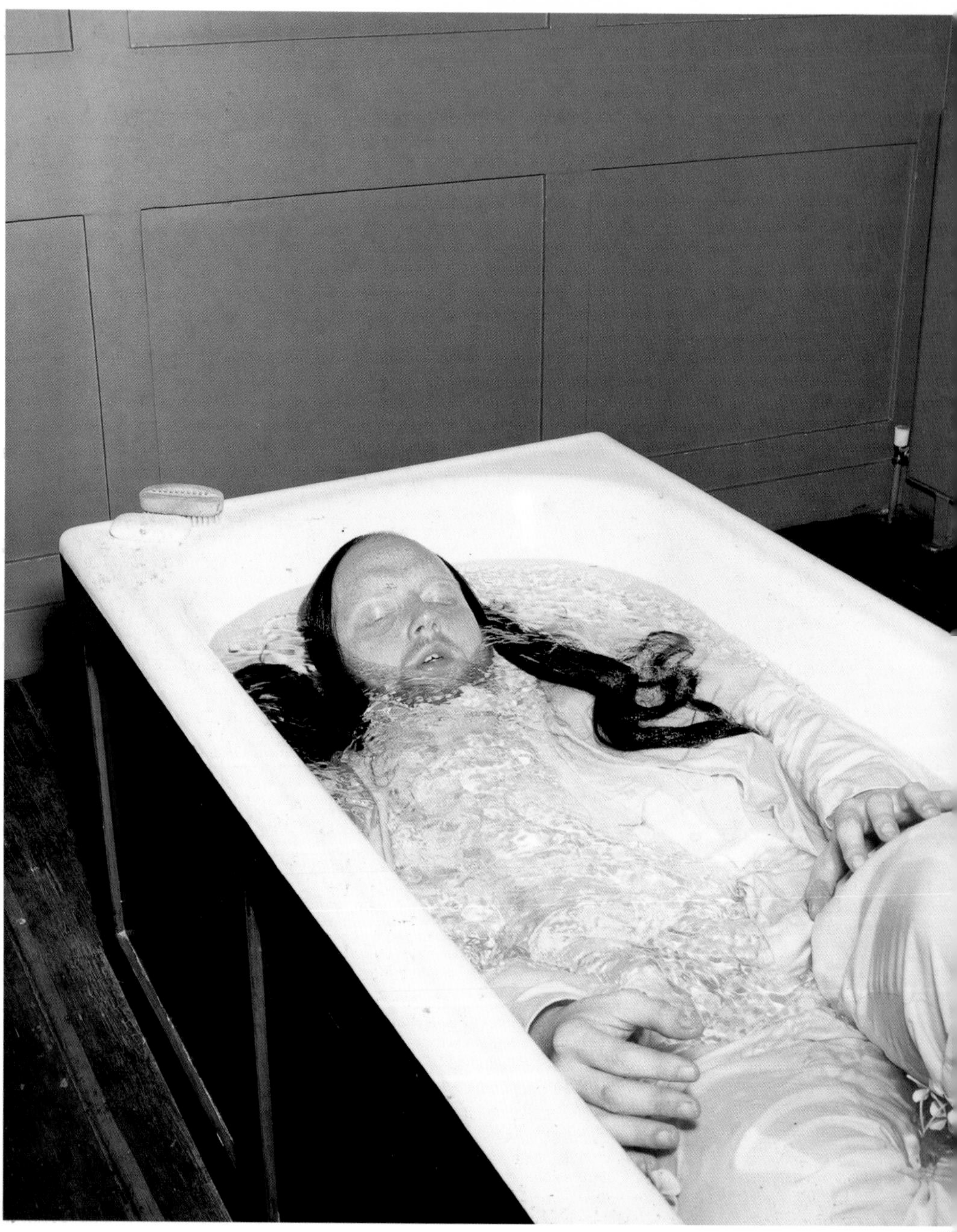

roger kelly

@ Nylon Gallery, London

felix lammers

styling: Carol Legrand
make-up: Yasmin
hair: Wendy Jles

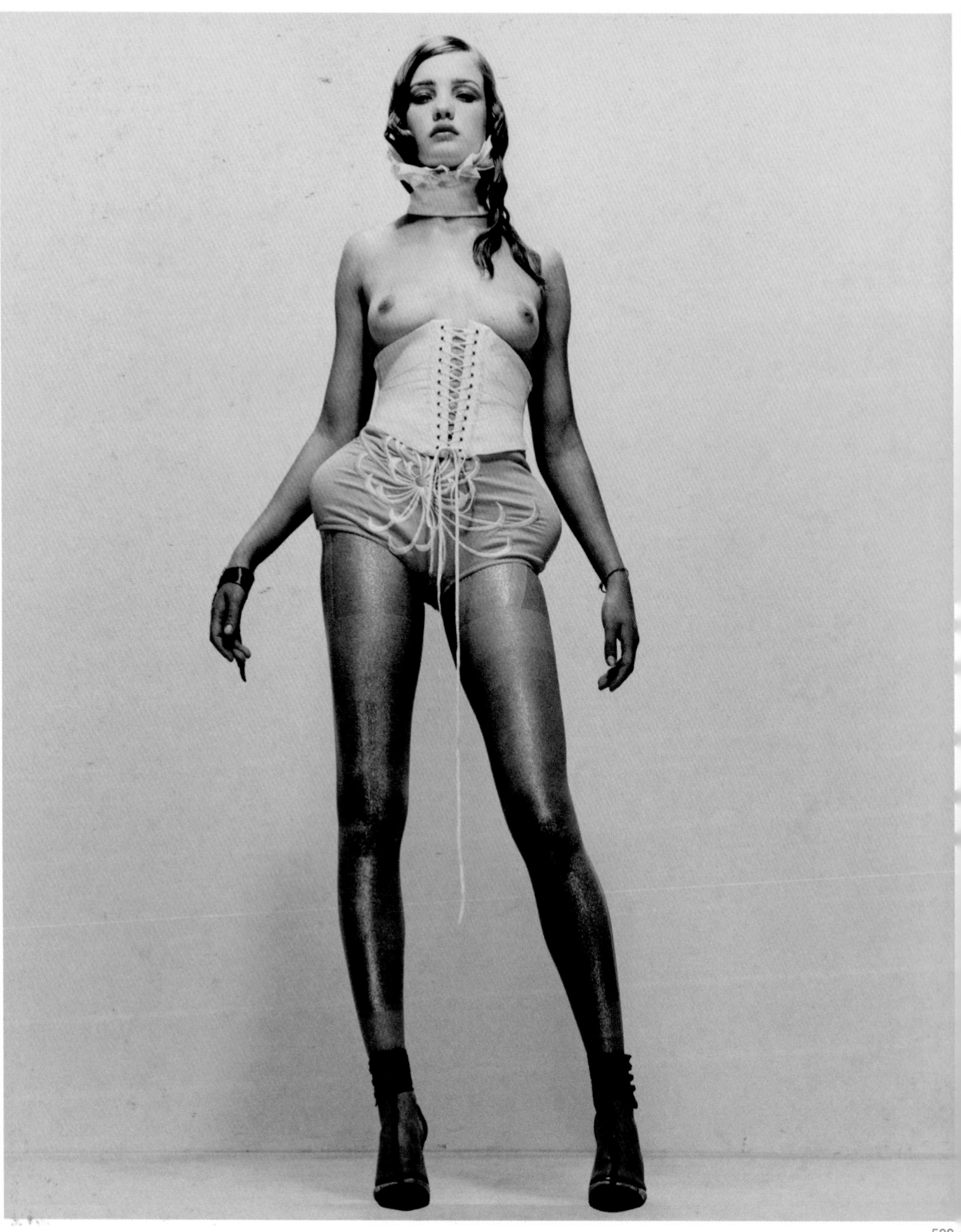

graeme montgomery + jo phillips

lee powers + bump

styling: Cynthia Lawrence-John
make-up: Kim Brown @ Rokit using Bobbi Brown
hair: George Ng-Yu-Tin

TV Shop
TV Shop
09867 236 578
our friendly operators are standing by to take your order

TV Shop
BVLGARI
18ct Gold 'premiere' necklace
Product 3005
£4,640.00
TV
09867 236 578
our friendly operators are standing by to take your order

TV Shop
BVLGARI
18ct Gold and Onyx Bracelet
Product 1589
£1,870.00
18ct Gold and Pavé Diamond old spiga Bracelet
Product 1580
£18,920.00
TV
09867 236 578
our friendly operators are standing by to take your order

TV Shop
Cartier
Necklace
18ct gold with diamonds
Product 3116
£14,150
Bracelet
18ct gold with diamonds
Product 3617
£9,275
TV
09867 236 578
our friendly operators are standing by to take your order

TV Shop

will sanders

styling: Nadine Sanders
make-up: Emma Williams
hair: Raphael Salley
model: Leanne Parsons @ Models 1

KEY SCIENCE for GCSE Chemistry
KEY SCIENCE for GCSE Chemistry
KEY SCIENCE for GCSE Chemistry

index

tank remains the most anti-professional magazine in the world. Its conception was partly a conceit and a response to the 'way things were done'. As well as being a maverick magazine, *tank* has also become one of the most influential. Its format, innovative editorial approach, design and feel have changed the magazine-publishing landscape. Uniquely, *tank* rejects the traditions of magazine publishing: culture of hype, blind celebrity worship and unconditional subservience to latent and blatant advertising demands. Above all, *tank* is a unique space for showcasing originality. Now that's original.

A good idea belongs to the world.